Container Gardens

SIMPLE STEPS
TO BEAUTIFUL POTTED PLANTS

TIME-LIFE BOOKS, ALEXANDRIA, VIRGINIA

TIME
LIFE

HOW-TO

Container
Gardens

Introduction

Growing plants in containers is the one gardening technique that works everywhere, for everyone. No matter what your climate, if you have the urge to garden, containers are your ally. They're appropriate for backyard greenhouses, rooftops, balconies, courtyards, sidewalks and stairs, and garden beds. Container gardening is so versatile that it serves collectors of rare plants as well as beginners. And it's easier than ever to find the materials you need. For growing everything from miniature to massive plants, today's pots come in a vast array of sizes and shapes.

Container plants are often the solution to garden problems. Where conditions are limited for in-ground planting, containers make gardening possible. Groupings of pots on a patio not only satisfy a green thumb, they also create an ambiance lacking in an unadorned landscape. Whether you choose flowers or foliage—pots of geraniums, a contoured boxwood, or an elaborate display of giant grasses and cannas—adding containers to your landscape softens the lines of a concrete slab or wood deck.

Gardening in containers gives you freedom to exercise your creativity. Just as one painter chooses to work in gentle watercolors while another prefers bold sweeps in acrylics or oils, you can easily and inexpensively experiment with plants, colors, and conditions. You can make a dramatic focal point at your doorway or merely fill a bare corner with color and scent. If a containerized plant doesn't harmonize smoothly in one location, simply move it to another. Containers can go nearly anywhere, from center stage to a quiet grouping in the wings. The options are limitless. 🌸

Getting Started

Today's containers are as exciting as the plants that grow in them. Choosing the right one means considering its construction and design, understanding the site it will occupy, and evaluating its harmony with the plants that will go in it. Once a container is planted, you'll want to keep your creation looking its best. Good maintenance practices go beyond basic watering and fertilizing to include frequent pruning and grooming. How much time you'll need to spend looking after your container garden depends on the type of pot and the plant species you choose.

As with any type of gardening, good cultural practices are the best safeguard against problems. Most trouble occurs when plants are potted in the wrong kind of soil, struggle in an incompatible site, or are improperly watered. By following the project guidelines, you'll avoid these pitfalls and enjoy many months or even years of success with container plants.

When it's time to move your plants from one pot to another, consult the steps outlined here, whether you're changing the soil, moving your plants up to a larger pot, or trimming roots. When you run into a snag, consult the troubleshooting section at the end of this section. ❧

Guide to Containers

So many types of containers fill the shelves in garden centers that it's possible to devote as much effort to choosing one as you do to selecting plants. The choice is easier when you divide the array into four basic types.

Porous pots make up the largest group. Terra-cotta pots, made from clay, allow air to move through the pot into the soil, promoting healthy roots. Clay absorbs water and allows evaporation. As a result, the soil dries out fairly rapidly, but plants are less likely to suffer from overwatering. The most durable and heaviest porous containers are concrete—favorite accents for formal gardens. Wood planters and tubs also fall into the porous category.

Nonporous plastic is the most inexpensive container material. Unlike terra cotta, plastic inhibits evaporation and blocks air from roots. It is therefore easy to overwater plants, making them prone to diseases and pests. Glazed ceramic and fiberglass pots are also nonporous.

For porches and balconies, wall pots and hanging baskets can be filled with graceful cascading and climbing plants.

And last, any number of items can double as pots. Attic treasures, garden paraphernalia, and flea-market finds can add a unique spark to your garden.

POROUS COLLECTION. *Terra-cotta and concrete pots come in many shapes and sizes. Porosity improves drainage and air circulation.*

NONPOROUS POTS. *These are durable and lightweight containers, good for plants that need extra moisture or that get moved around.*

HANGING BASKETS. *Install hanging baskets and wall pots of cascading plants to accent a porch or to decorate where space is limited.*

OFFBEAT POTS. *Antique and unusual pots add whimsy. If you can't add drainage holes, just set the nursery pot right inside the container.*

HERE'S HOW
MOVING CONTAINERS

Relocating a large pot or planter box filled with moist potting mix and plants is heavy work, calling for extra hands and special equipment. One of the safest ways to tackle the job is with a sturdy dolly or hand truck outfitted with large wheels and a long lip to support the container.

You can manage short-distance moves by using a makeshift sled. Tip a container to one side and slide a section of plywood or a durable tarp underneath. Rotate the pot or box from side to side until it rests on the "sled," and then pull it along the ground to its new location.

Three pipes or wooden dowels make a handy tool for moving heavy planter boxes. Rock the containers so that you can slip two dowels under the planter, then slowly roll the planter forward onto the third dowel. When the rear dowel is free, bring it to the front and keep rolling the planter forward. Continue this pattern until you get to the new location.

Preparing and Repairing Containers

PREVENTING ROT. *To prevent rot, apply two coats of wood sealant to the inside of a clean wood container. Seal or paint the outside.*

The ideal container blends practicality, function, and artistry. When you select a pot, it's important to choose a container that best suits the plants that will grow in it. A container that is too large or too small stresses the plants it holds; stressed plants are more susceptible to pests and diseases, are often less attractive, and live shorter lives.

Take into account the site your container will occupy. Your plants need certain conditions to thrive. Most critical is to place them where they will get the right amount of sun. The container you choose can also affect these conditions. For example, clay pots in hot, sunny spots dry out quickly; dark-colored plastic pots may overheat; and soil in glazed pots may dry out too slowly. Choose containers with the plants' needs in mind. Experiment a little and your container garden can look beautiful all season long.

Above all, remember that plants grow best and stay healthiest when provided even moisture and good drainage. So be prepared to drill or puncture holes in any pot you have or purchase that doesn't already have them.

If your favorite container should happen to break, you can often repair it instead of discarding it. One of the easiest types of containers to repair is terra cotta, provided it isn't in tiny pieces. Waterproof epoxy and masking tape are usually all you need. Cracked pots can be reinforced with a flexible wire wrap, and the cracks you can't fix can be disguised. Grow cascading plants in chipped pots so the foliage hides the imperfections.

When you have chosen a container, take a few steps to prepare it as shown here. Renewing old pots and readying new ones will pay off in the end. ❦

HAVE ON HAND:

▶ Paintbrush

▶ Wood sealant

▶ Bucket

▶ Drill

▶ Waterproof epoxy

▶ Masking tape

▶ Flexible wire

REPAIRING BROKEN POTS. *Salvage a clay pot with waterproof epoxy. Clean the pieces, glue them, and bind with masking tape until dry.*

PREPARING CLAY POTS. *Soak new terra-cotta pots for 30 minutes before planting, as dry pots draw needed moisture out of soil.*

ENSURING DRAINAGE. *In solid-bottom pots use a power drill and a ⅜-inch masonry bit to bore one or more holes in the bottom.*

REPAIRING CRACKED POTS. *Wrap flexible wire under the rim, twisting ends together tightly. Add wire around the base if needed.*

HIDING CRACKS. *Conceal cracks and chips with arching and trailing stems or plants with large leaves.*

HERE'S HOW

REUSING CONTAINERS

Renew old pots by scraping off salt residues from hard water and fertilizers. Use a stiff brush on rough pots, a kitchen scrubber on smooth ones.

Control disease pathogens by washing pots in a 9:1 solution of water and household bleach. Rinse thoroughly before planting.

For an interchangeable display, set a plain nursery container inside a decorative pot. Use bricks or blocks, if needed, to elevate and support the plant inside the container.

Containers in the Landscape

Container gardens are a natural choice when space is at a premium. In cities, window boxes are often a gardener's only outlet, as well as a way to beautify the neighborhood. A plain entryway, no matter how tiny, can be made instantly warmer and more welcoming with the addition of a favorite planting. A splash of botanical color in a decorative container can brighten up any location in your yard, whatever the soil conditions.

When space is not an issue, use containers as the perfect technique for showcasing a treasured plant in the garden. A dramatic yucca with its arching, sword-shaped leaves and towering flower stem cannot be missed in a large terra-cotta pot on a sunny patio, but it could be overshadowed by flashier foliage in a shrub border.

Whether you're featuring just one plant or grouping several together, consider the requisites of the site. Take into account the amount of rain your potted plants will receive, their exposure to sun and shade, the force of prevailing winds, and any impact from pets or wildlife. In addition to these factors, consider the size of the container and how readily it loses or holds moisture.

Once you know the conditions your plants will face, turn to the suitability of plants for container growing. Plants that shun crowding are best grown in the ground. Extremely fast or slow growers may be unsuitable in pots, particularly in combination. But nearly every type of plant has a representative that enjoys container culture. You may need to experiment a bit before you find just the right one for the design you have in mind. In fact, much of the fun and challenge of container gardening is attempting to find the right combinations of plants for a particular space.

You'll also want to consider how to balance the amount of flowers and foliage and how to achieve pleasing contrasts of size and texture, as well as the overall impression of a plant grouping.

Coordinating colors in mixed plantings can be a challenge, especially if you purchase and pot annuals and perennials before they come into bloom. So be ready to improvise and substitute one plant for another during the growing season.

Finally, know the care requirements of each of the plants you choose. You may need to fit some extra time into your schedule to care for high-maintenance plants in containers. 🌸

A GOOD SOLUTION. *Plant in pots to solve problems of difficult soil and bad drainage. Elevate pots to allow drainage underneath.*

EVENING DRAMA. *Dress up patios for evening enjoyment: Plant a variety of large white flowers with sweet scents.*

A WARM WELCOME. *Add welcoming décor and a touch of formality to entries with fragrant and evergreen plants.*

WINDOW BOX CHARM. *Enjoy bright color from inside and outside your home. Choose long bloomers and cascades of foliage.*

PLANTER BOXES. *Rely on foliage plants for planter boxes in outdoor living areas. As the seasons come and go, fill in with spots of color.*

A SPLASH OF COLOR. *Perk up a plain landscape with colorful annuals. When plants are at their prime, move pots into the spotlight.*

HERE'S HOW

VALUABLE SCENTS

Do a little testing before relying on general statements about a plant's fragrance. Some herbs are wonderfully aromatic only when they are crushed. Thyme and chamomile make soft, aromatic carpets on garden paths as footsteps release their scent. But trailing over the edge of a clay pot, these plants rest quietly without releasing their scent. Similarly, one species or variety of plant may be scentless, whereas another is strongly perfumed.

To enjoy a certain fragrance in a containerized planting, feature it in an individual pot. Subtle scents of lavender, for example, may be overpowered in close proximity to stronger aromas.

Potting Mixes

Light and porous potting mixes are the cornerstone of every successful container garden. Whether you plant in a hanging basket or a half-barrel tub, you'll want a growing medium that drains freely and allows good airflow but also retains moisture. Of the various formulas for creating a potting mix, all are made up of ingredients with these features.

Most mixes contain very little, if any, soil. Garden soil is never recommended for containers because it often becomes compacted and may contain pests and diseases. The mixes you can purchase or make are loosely referred to as potting soil, although they're actually soilless.

Certain situations call for specialty mixes. Succulents and cacti need fast-draining mixes with generous quantities of sand and perlite. Acid-loving plants prefer shredded bark; shade plants prosper with some vermiculite.

Although most mixes can be used interchangeably in various containers, a few precautions are in order. Reserve vermiculite for plants needing constant supplies of moisture, and use it only in small containers, as it tends to compact in large pots and restrict drainage. The same is true for water-absorbent polymers that hold many times their weight in water and release it slowly as the potting mix dries. They are invaluable in containers that dry out quickly and with plants that depend on moist soil, but they hold water so well that they can promote root rot in plants grown in nonporous pots, as well as in plants that prefer dry conditions.

If you need potting mix for just a few containers it is often easier to purchase a ready-made potting mix. But when working with numerous pots or very large ones, it's much more economical to buy in bulk or make your own. The recipes here provide basic mixes easy to adapt for a wide range of planting options. ❧

FOR A BASIC MIX. *Combine equal parts peat moss, compost, and perlite. Use a tub for small amounts and a tarp for a large volume.*

FOR DRY-CLIMATE PLANTS. *Combine 1 part basic mix, 1 part compost, 2 parts sand.*

HAVE ON HAND:

▶ Plastic tub or tarp

▶ Peat moss

▶ Compost

▶ Perlite

▶ Limestone

▶ Sand

▶ Shredded bark

▶ Vermiculite

Lightly moisten and mix with a trowel or shovel until all ingredients are evenly blended.

For each gallon of mix add 1 tablespoon granular limestone. Blend thoroughly until all ingredients are uniformly mixed.

HERE'S HOW

MIXING LARGE QUANTITIES

To prepare a large quantity of potting mix, construct a pile on a hard, clean surface, such as a paved driveway, or on a tarp spread on the lawn. A shovel with a large blade, such as a grain or snow shovel, is a handy mixing tool. As you turn the mix, add small amounts of water to lightly dampen the ingredients.

When preparing a potting mix yourself, wait until you're ready to plant to add fertilizer.

FOR ACID-LOVING PLANTS. *Combine 1 part basic mix, 1 part peat moss, 1 part shredded bark.*

FOR SHADE-LOVING PLANTS. *Combine 2 parts basic mix, 1 part vermiculite, 1 part peat moss.*

Potting and Repotting

Whether you begin with several small vegetable seedlings or a more mature shrub, there are similarities in how you go about potting them.

Root systems are equally important on all plants and require careful consideration at planting time. Ideally, roots like to be spread out loosely in all directions so they are never crowded. But as they branch and grow, roots tend to become matted and wrapped around the rootball while still in their nursery pots. When it's impossible to separate compacted roots at planting or repotting time, don't hesitate to cut into the rootball in order to spread the roots out. New roots will grow quickly as soon as they're set into fresh, moist soil.

Take some time to prepare before you launch into a planting project. Line up new plant purchases and do a survey of your current container garden to determine how many plants need repotting. If you have a sizable collection, it will be easiest to repot a group of them at once, since it's a messy job. Have all the materials you need on hand, and prepare a shaded area where the newly potted plants can rest before you move them into a sunny spot.

PREPARING PLANTS

Spring and early summer are the ideal times to plant and repot, since these are the seasons when plant growth is strongest and when roots regenerate quickly. Now is a good time to clear away yellowed foliage and trim back excess growth. You'll end up with a smaller plant that will be easier to handle during potting, and the reduced foliage will put less demand on a stressed root system. If you are working with a perennial, determine whether it needs to be divided at this time.

Check the condition of bare-root plants the day before you pot them. If you've bought them from a mail-order supplier, follow accompanying directions; otherwise, soak them for at least one hour before planting. It may be necessary to soak very dry roots overnight. Trim any rootlets that remain shriveled.

At least an hour before you begin, water plants thoroughly and allow the soil to drain. If a rootball is exceedingly dry, submerge it in water and allow it to soak for half an hour. During the potting process, roots are damaged least when in contact with moist soil. 🌺

To remove a plant from its nursery container, support the rootball as you invert the pot. Avoid lifting by the stem, which causes breakage.

Tap the rim against a hard surface if you have difficulty removing a plant. If the plant still won't budge, carefully cut the container away.

Use your fingers or a tool, such as a three-tined hand fork, to tease roots loose all around the rootball. Trim off any long, coiled roots.

Slice through the rootball on all four sides to loosen severely bound roots. Make the cut at least 1 inch deep.

PLANTING

For optimum health, pot plants initially with an inch of moist soil between the container and rootball. This allows enough space for the root system to expand for at least one year. If you allow too much soil, it will hold more moisture than plants can readily absorb, and in soggy conditions, roots will rot. Work additional soil between each rootball that you add to a container, taking care to firm each plant in place as you go. Strive to achieve good soil-to-root contact while at the same time avoiding compaction.

When you are combining plants of different sizes, place the one with the largest root-

ball first, before completely filling the container with potting mix. Water it slightly to allow for settling before adding smaller plants. When you finish, all should be at the same level as they were growing in their nursery pots.

Some nursery plants need special attention. For bare-root plants, form a mound of potting mix in the container, set the plant on top so the crown will be just above the finished soil level, and spread the roots out evenly. Plants that are purchased balled and burlapped must be set in a depression with soil all around. Cut and remove all wire and ties, and when the plant is in place, slip the wrapping out from underneath. Also remove paper pulp and mesh netting from plants of any size. These temporary containers can restrict root growth and interfere with watering when they're left intact. 🌿

HAVE ON HAND:

▶ Container
▶ Trowel
▶ Potting mix

Fill a container with premoistened potting mix. Poke your fingers into soil to lightly settle the potting mix.

Pull back the soil and set the plant at the same depth it was in the nursery container.

Position plants close together. Press soil gently around each rootball to remove large air pockets.

Leave a 1-inch space below the rim for watering in small pots; leave 2 inches in larger pots.

REPOTTING

Knowing when to repot is key to growing healthy plants. Fast-growing species or those that have lived in the same container for more than a year may be potbound. Check the rootball when growth becomes rampant or, conversely, when it slows or stops during the growing season, or when the rootball is pushed above the rim. Move these plants to a larger container, or trim their roots and replant in the same pot. Remember, though, that some plants, such as lavender and clivia, grow best in pots that would be too small for other similar-sized plants. You can restrict the size of many large perennials, shrubs, and trees by confining their growing space and keeping them in the same container year after year. But to encourage a small plant to grow larger, you'll need to repot it each year in a slightly larger container.

As you pot a plant, take note of its strength. If stems appear weak, give them a supporting trellis or tie them to a bamboo stake. Leave the support to be camouflaged by dense foliage or remove it in several weeks after the plant is established.

Some plants are so slow growing that repotting is necessary only after many years. However, these plants benefit from an annual top dressing. Remove the topmost 1 to 2 inches of soil, taking care not to dislodge any roots. Replace it with the same potting mix originally used or a mix enriched with compost. ❧

HAVE ON HAND:

▶ Cloth strips
▶ Container
▶ Tape measure
▶ Pruning shears
▶ Scrubber or sponge
▶ Potting mix

Repot plants every 1 to 2 years. Wrap foliage with cloth strips before removing plant from pot.

When you select a new container, use one that is no more than 2 inches wider than the original pot.

Trim 1 to 2 inches off the rootball of large plants. Scrub the container to remove salt residues, and repot.

Freshen soil with the same type mix. Set plant on a new layer of soil and fill around the rootball.

Watering and Fertilizing

How much to water depends largely on the weather. Cool, overcast days and summer rains reduce the need for supplemental moisture, whereas long spells of wind and sun may call for watering twice a day. Keep in mind that containers on covered patios and under roof overhangs rarely benefit from light rain showers and therefore stay drier. You'll need to check them more frequently than those in more exposed sites. To avoid overly wet conditions that contribute to root rot, always probe the top few inches of the soil with your finger to test for moisture.

The best time to water plants is early in the morning, when the temperature is cool and the sunlight soft. Watering late in the afternoon means roots stay wet all night, fostering disease problems, and watering in harsh afternoon light can damage tender leaves. Use a watering can with a long spout or a hose with a wand attachment and breaker to put the water right where your plants need it—on the soil.

The size of the container, the material it's made of, and the type of potting mix used also have a bearing on how often you need to water. Small pots dry out faster than large ones, and unglazed clay pots lose water more rapidly than glazed pots and those made of other nonporous materials. Fast-draining mixes with perlite retain less water than those with vermiculite and compost. Peat moss holds water for longer periods than sand, but once it dries out, it may repel rather than absorb moisture. The best safeguard against so many variables is to check containers daily during the growing season.

In addition to frequent watering, plants in containers need frequent fertilizing to stay vigorous and healthy. To maintain rich foliage color and a long season of flowering, mix in a slow-release fertilizer at planting time to provide roots with a steady supply of nutrients. Unlike in-ground plants, whose roots can grow out and down in search of nutrients, those in containers must get all their nourishment from what's in the potting mix in addition to any extra that you provide.

Even with slow-release fertilizer, be ready to treat your container plants periodically with light doses of a liquid fertilizer to sustain strong growth and heavy flowering. Watch for signs of overfertilizing, however. If you observe tip burn on leaf margins or a heavy buildup of salt deposits on pots, cut back on fertilizing. ❦

TEST THE SOIL. *Add water when the soil in the container is dry about an inch or two below the surface.*

AUTOMATED WATERING SYSTEM. *This gives you the freedom to travel while maintaining a well-watered garden.*

HOSE WATERING. *Use an aluminum wand with shutoff and water breaker to water plants, gently rinse foliage, and increase humidity.*

APPLYING FERTILIZER. *Sprinkle slow-release pellets evenly and well away from the stem. Be sure no pellets are lodged in foliage.*

PROTECT SURFACES. *Water can discolor surfaces, and fertilizer salts can corrode them. Protect surfaces by placing saucers under pots.*

DRY AND WET. *Many plants like moist roots and dry leaves; to water, set pots in a shallow tub of tepid water for 30 to 60 minutes; drain well.*

HERE'S HOW

FERTILIZER KNOW-HOW

Complete fertilizers contain nitrogen, phosphorus, and potassium (N, P, K)—three key elements needed by plants. All these nutrients are best supplied gradually, as an overabundance is not only wasteful but can actually injure or kill plants.

It's important to know that although nitrogen is critical for plant growth, it promotes foliage more than flowering. Phosphorus plays a greater role in bloom production, and potassium is needed for overall vigor of plants. Three numbers on the label, such as 5-10-10, indicate the percentage of nitrogen, phosphorus, and potassium, in that order.

When using liquid fertilizers, apply light doses frequently, because soluble materials easily leach away and are lost. Use fractional doses when applying foliar sprays to avoid damaging sensitive leaves.

Pruning and Grooming

One of the great advantages of container gardening is the convenience it affords in managing your plants. Instead of getting down on hands and knees, you can pull up a bench or stool when it's time to prune and groom. Because plants in containers are usually on display for closeup viewing, you will want to maintain them in top condition.

Timely grooming not only keeps up appearances but also ensures bountiful blooms. By removing faded flowers, you encourage a plant to rebloom again and again. This applies to annuals and perennials, for the most part, but deadheading will prolong blossoming in some flowering shrubs, as well. In some cases, all you need to do is pinch off a blossom at its base, but for plants that bloom on elongated stems, you'll need to trim the stem just above a leaf.

Leave a few flowers on your plants if you want to collect seed for planting next year or if you have plants with decorative seed heads, such as scabiosa, gazania, and clematis.

Besides deadheading, regular grooming calls for removing excess and crowded growth. When you combine several different plant species in the same pot, it's inevitable at some point that one will overtake its neighbor. Judicious thinning maintains balance in a container and allows air to circulate around the foliage, preventing fungal disease.

Check plants on a weekly basis, noting their changes as you make your watering rounds. In general, groom frequently, but prune less often. An exception is when training young plants to assume an upright or sculptural shape, as most pruning controls size or directs growth. Sometimes this means removing woody branches to the base to stimulate new sprouts or rejuvenate a neglected plant. As you prune, remember that topping, or shearing the topmost growth, encourages branching, while thinning reduces overly dense growth.

At season's end, discard annual plants and cut back perennials. Mulch less hardy perennials with bark chips or pine boughs after the ground freezes. ❧

DEADHEADING. *Use scissors to cut back, or deadhead, faded blossoms. Regular deadheading keeps plants tidy and encourages longer flowering.*

HAVE ON HAND:

▶ Scissors

▶ Pruning shears

▶ Hedge shears

FORCING GROWTH. *On leggy plants, cut back stems just above a lower bud to force vigorous shoots and more compact growth.*

TIDYING UP. *Remove dead and yellowed foliage to keep plants neat as well as healthy. Check foliage for signs of pests or disease.*

PINCHING BACK. *As young plants grow, pinch off tender tips with fingers to induce fullness; use small shears on tough stems.*

SHEARING. *Use hedge shears to trim potted shrubs into formal shapes. Shear just the tips of new growth.*

THINNING. *Thin out crowded growth in the centers of roses and other shrubs to improve appearance and to encourage new branching.*

HERE'S HOW

PROLONGING BLOOM

As flowers edge past their peak, pinch or clip them off where they are attached to the stem. Be sure to remove the entire flower—not just the petals—so that no seeds form. Seed formation inhibits additional flowering.

On cascading plants such as sweet alyssum or lobelia, trim back the entire plant by one-half or more when blossoming wanes. This forces out new stems, keeps growth in check, and improves appearance.

On shrubs, flowering generally occurs during a few weeks in one season only. However, you can prolong blossoming on many species by deadheading faded blooms promptly.

Troubleshooting

By following sound gardening practices and avoiding extremes, you will encounter few problems. Watering alone accounts for most plant woes. Too much water leads to soggy soil, yellowed foliage, and root rot. Too little moisture causes wilting, browned leaves, and stunting. Both conditions stress and weaken plants, leaving them prey to pests and diseases. Timing is also important. Watering early in the day allows foliage to dry more quickly, forestalling fungal diseases.

Insects regularly visit outdoor plants, though most never cause serious injury. If you discover aphids, leafhoppers, spider mites, thrips, or whiteflies, try washing them off with a strong spray from your hose—the easiest way to dislodge and discourage them. In some cases, you will need to hose off plants repeatedly. Larger insects can be knocked or picked off and destroyed.

If you do choose to use a pesticide, it is vital that you follow label directions exactly. Toxic materials pose considerable risks for people and pets, and the margin for error is small. Because container plants tend to be near outdoor living areas, it's a good idea to begin problem solving with the least toxic material. If plain water doesn't work, try a soap spray (in a ratio of 1 tablespoon soap to 1 cup water) or a biological treatment, such as Bt, before resorting to any more toxic chemicals.

Keep in mind that overall plant health results from a multitude of factors. When you first select a plant, know its tolerance for stress and its suitability for your climate. For example, some plants demand dry air, while others depend on high humidity. Too much wind, heat, cold, or rough handling can cause foliage to brown. Check plants every week in summer for the angle and intensity of the sun. You may need to protect them from reflected heat at one point in the growing season and from damaging frosts at another. And before placing containers in shaded sites, know the shade tolerance of each plant. ❧

HAVE ON HAND:

- ▶ Spray bottle
- ▶ 16:1 water-to-soap solution
- ▶ 9:1 water-to-bleach solution
- ▶ Fungicide
- ▶ Light-colored container

SUCKING PESTS. *Hose off aphids and other sucking pests such as mealybugs, whiteflies, and mites. Use a soap spray for persistent problems.*

ROOT ROT. *If foliage becomes limp and yellow, inspect soil for root rot (water-soaked areas on roots). Let soil dry out thoroughly.*

HARMLESS ANTS. *Ants do not harm plants but are attracted to honeydew excreted by sucking insects. Spray with water or soap solution.*

LARGE INSECTS. *Pick off slugs and other large insects that you find. Destroy pests by crushing or dropping in a mild bleach solution.*

LEAF PROBLEMS. *To control leaf diseases, plant disease-resistant varieties, apply a fungicide, or move plants to a bright, breezy spot.*

TOO MUCH SUN. *Plants in black containers can overheat in bright sun. Repot plants in a lighter-colored container.*

HERE'S HOW

IDENTIFYING PESTS

If you suspect that a pest is present but you can't see it, look for identifying signs and symptoms, then use a hand lens to examine both the upper and lower surfaces of leaves.

Thrips may be present if new foliage is puckered and bronzed and petals are lopsided and brown.

Spider mites may be the culprits if the foliage has tiny yellow dots or if you see webbing.

Black sooty mold forms a sugary excretion (called honeydew) that sucking insects, such as aphids and scale insects, deposit on plants. If you see ants feeding on honeydew, look for these plant pests.

Spittlebugs create foamy bubbles on stems at a leaf base. Spray these off with a hose or knock them off by hand and destroy them.

Seasonal Gardens

Versatility is one of the great appeals of container gardening. Pot size, plant varieties, and seasonal performance promise garden rewards for terraces, decks, and balconies at any time of year. You can adapt your container garden to fit into a complex planting scheme or to stand alone. When a favorite plant looks its best, you can move it in closer so that you may enjoy every minute of its seasonal finery.

Container gardens invite special attractions each season. In spring, you can fill pots with early bloomers and place them outside windows or tuck them into sprouting garden beds to fill in empty spots. After several weeks, it's easy to transform the potted garden to a summer theme, and then as the months progress, to autumn and winter expressions.

The projects in this section lead you through the year, suggesting ways to create nine different potted gardens in four seasons. Versatility plays a part in every project. With bulbs, you have the choice of storing the planted pot and repeating a favorite performance next year, or storing the bulbs separately and using the container for a new combination. Other projects are designed for one or two seasons only. Summer offers the greatest number of possibilities, whether you choose flowering annuals or vegetables and herbs. By selecting plants that work best in your locale, you can enjoy a spectacular container again and again. ❦

Early Spring Bulbs and Flowers

Spring flowers have a way of dismissing the final days of winter. They appeal not only to our senses but also to our vision of things to come, promising long months of scent and color. Bulbs and flowers in containers concentrate that effect. Bright color is key to their impact, but more important is a selection of hardy species that will hold up in unpredictable spring weather. Overnight frosts and chilling rains are not a problem for the plants featured here. They can tolerate the tough transition from winter to spring beautifully.

Maintaining a blooming container presents few demands in spring. Cool days and nights cut down on the need for frequent watering, and moderate temperatures prolong the bloom period as well, which means you won't have to worry about constant deadheading.

The plants in this arrangement will remain bright and vibrant for many weeks, but you may want to lift them for planting in the garden after their blooms have gone. If any of the species are unavailable to you, be adventuresome and choose a similar substitute. Most types of pansies and spring-flowering bulbs would be perfectly at home here. ✿

A SPRING BOUQUET

Combine a minimum of five to seven bulbs of each type for brilliant splashes of color in a mixed bulb planting. Group each species together, placing bulbs so they touch one another. Set taller varieties in the center or back of the pot; keep low growers in front. Try to balance your color scheme and include some flowering annuals in colors that are compatible with the bulbs.

HAVE ON HAND:

- 18 x 18-inch pot (lobster pot)
- Drill and bit
- Mesh onion bags
- Styrofoam peanuts
- Potting mix
- Drying screen

Plants

- 5–7 tulips in bud or bloom

- 5–7 narcissus or daffodils in bud or bloom
- 4–5 pansies
- 4–5 striped squill or grape hyacinth
- 3–4 Greek windflowers
- 3–4 ivy or periwinkle sprigs

Drill drainage holes in bottom of large container if needed. Fill 2 or 3 mesh onion bags with Styrofoam peanuts and place in container.

Fill with moist, soilless potting mix to within 2 inches of top. Plant budding tulips near the back of the container.

Position the narcissus or daffodils in two clumps in front of the tulips.

In front of the tulips and narcissus or daffodils, plant an array of colorful pansies. Dark violet varieties work well here, but any color will do nicely.

Fill in with extra potting mix as you work, always keeping the surface about 1 inch below the rim of the container.

Position several small-bulbed spring flowers, such as striped squill or grape hyacinth, close to the sides; add a few Greek windflowers.

You can also add a few sprigs of trailing ground cover, such as ivy or periwinkle, to the edge of the pot.

After the foliage dies back, lift bulbs from pot, trim off leaves, and place on screen to dry. Replant bulbs in the fall.

HERE'S HOW

INCREASING BULBS

Keep watering and feeding your bulbs until the foliage dies back, then lift them out of the container. You can separate any new bulbs (called offsets or bulblets) joined to the old ones and replant them. Large offsets make the biggest flowers; very small ones may need another year or two of growth before they become productive.

Corms shrivel up after a year in the ground, and new ones form on the top. Like bulblets, small cormels that grow at the sides of corms eventually will flower. You can divide rhizomes and tuberous roots like iris and dahlias to increase their numbers. However, tubers like cyclamen cannot be divided.

Alternatives

SPRING-FLOWERING SHRUBS

Flowering shrubs are prized in spring for the freshness and beauty of their exuberant blooms. While some grow too large for container culture, many species include a variety small enough to be suitable. Large shrubs grow best in wooden tubs or boxes, but dwarf varieties thrive in smaller pots. After blossoming subsides, move them to the background and highlight containers of summer flowers.

Azaleas and dwarf rhododendrons (shown here) stand out as two favorites. Lavish blooms cover their branch tips in an astonishing array of colors. Choose a variety for its bloom time and color tones so that it is compatible with nearby plants. For color over several months, plant early, midseason, and late varieties.

No matter which spring-blooming shrub you select, take blossom shape and foliage texture into account. For example, pieris and drooping leucothoe both bear gracefully arched stems of urn-shaped flowers that are beautifully displayed against glossy, leathery foliage. Pea-shaped flowers of the various brooms completely smother their thin branches. And camellia's symmetrical blossoms, which vary from single petals to ruffly doubles, stand in sharp contrast to layers of dark, shiny leaves. ❧

SPRING-FLOWERING PERENNIALS

The joy of perennials lies in witnessing their return to full glory year after year. Spring bloomers generate great excitement because they usher in a new gardening year. So profuse are their numbers, however, that choosing just a few is difficult. For the container gardener, it's best to stay away from those that need space for deep or fast-spreading roots and focus instead on well-behaved perennials that don't grow out of bounds in a single season. It's also rewarding to choose repeat bloomers known for extended flowering.

Display your perennials individually, or combine them in large containers. Potted alone, grassy clumps of aubretia, sea pinks, and cheddar pinks develop into charming little hummocks supporting an abundance of small, delicate blossoms that dot the foliage. Planted under taller plants, such mounds spill over the edge of a pot, obscuring the rim with their cascading foliage. Bleeding heart (shown here) trembles gracefully over the pot below. Bright white candytuft and blue forget-me-nots, the many-hued primroses, and long-blooming nemesia are other spring favorites. Be sure to include coral bells if you're looking for a multiuse perennial. Long after the tall flower spikes finish, clumps of mottled foliage impress until fall. ❧

A Bouquet of Tulips

Although there are many lovely summer and fall types, we associate bulbs with spring. Happily, they are well suited to container culture, adapting easily to either shallow bulb pots or deeper tubs and boxes. You can treat bulbs grown in containers much the same as those grown in the ground. For the most eye-catching designs, plant them in masses of a single variety or large groups of the same color.

Bulbs are one of the easiest and most satisfying kinds of plants to grow. By starting with firm, healthy bulbs and planting in loose, well-drained soil with fertilizer mixed in where the roots will grow, you will be on your way to producing a vibrant bulb garden.

How you handle bulbs after they finish blooming depends, for the most part, on the space you have for storage and for gardening. You can remove the bulbs from the container, wipe the soil from them, and store them in bags or boxes; or you can store the entire pot, bulbs and all. If you lack storage space, leave the bulbs in deep pots and plant over the top of them with summer annuals, just as you would in a garden bed. Be warned, however, that this method may damage bulbs that prefer to stay dry during dormancy. ❦

MASSING BULBS

Plant long-lived tulips, such as Darwin hybrids, if you want to reuse the bulbs in pots or the garden next year. To stagger bloom over several weeks, plant a combination of early- and late-blooming varieties of similar color and shape.

For a formal effect, prepare identical pots with bulbs arranged in the same pattern. As the bulbs come into bloom, set the pots on opposite sides of an entry door or walkway, or at the top or base of a stairway. ❧

HAVE ON HAND:

▶ 16-inch-wide x 12-inch-deep terra-cotta pot

▶ Potting mix

▶ Slow-release fertilizer

▶ Pruning shears

Plants

▶ 20–25 tulip bulbs

Cover the bottom of a pot 16 inches wide by 12 inches deep with 2 inches of soilless potting mix.

Arrange a layer of bulbs, pointed ends up. Set bulbs 1 inch apart.

Cover the bulbs with a layer of potting mix so the soil is about 5 inches from the rim of the pot. Add an application of slow-release fertilizer.

Add a final layer of bulbs, pressing them gently into the soil. Cover bulbs with potting mix to about 1 inch of the rim. Add more slow-release fertilizer.

Water lightly. Move the pot to a place that remains 40° to 50°F; store 8 to 12 weeks. If soil dries out, moisten slightly.

When shoots appear, move the pot to a place where it receives at least 6 hours of sun a day. Keep soil moist but not wet.

Cut out flowering stems as blossoms wilt and fade. Allow foliage to flourish, which helps rejuvenate bulbs for next year.

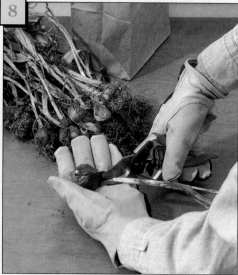

Lift bulbs and dry. Clip off foliage and store bulbs in a cool, dry location until it is time to replant in the fall.

HERE'S HOW

BULBS IN CONTAINERS

Planting bulbs in containers differs somewhat from planting in the ground. Bulbs can be set much closer in pots, even touching each other. In climates where freezing occurs, bulbs should not touch the pot—keep some soil around the sides of the container for insulation.

During storage, bulbs may grow roots but should not be allowed to put out top growth until spring. To maintain bulbs in a semidormant state, store them between 40° and 50°F until danger of a freeze has passed.

When combining bulbs with different bloom times in the same container, plant the later-flowering species or varieties on the cooler bottom; plant the earlier bloomers in the upper layers.

Choose small bulbs or miniature varieties to plant under trees and shrubs in containers. Spring starflower is a good choice for its profuse blooms and rapid spread. After its leaves brown and bulbs are dormant, overplant an annual ground cover.

Alternatives

A SINGLE SPECIMEN

You don't have to be a collector to show off your favorite bulbs in a classic fashion. Simply pot them up, with one or more to a terra-cotta pot or bowl. Though plain and simple, this artful planting has a dramatic impact that is hard to beat when in full bloom. And because many bulbs are fragrant, their scents have greater impact en masse. Be sure to place the container where it can be easily approached and viewed.

Groupings of 6-inch containers show off bulbs to wonderful advantage. This size pot is easy to move around from display area to tabletop to garden bed.

For the best effect, plant five hyacinth bulbs (shown here) to a 6-inch pot with their points just above the soil level. When planting other bulbs in small pots, set them at least an inch under the soil. Plant only three double daffodils and other narcissus per pot—more if they are smaller. Plant 10 to 12 oxalis, grape hyacinth, Dutch crocus, and glory-of-the-snow. A 6-inch pot will accommodate six to eight snowdrops but only one Cuban lily. Most of these bulbs stand alone quite nicely, but for those tall stems that appear weak, slip in a single-stem bulb support or tie stems to a thin bamboo cane. ✺

BULBLIKE PLANTS

Bulblike plants are similar to true bulbs in that they, too, undergo a lengthy dormancy. These include plants that grow from corms (modified stems), tubers (short, swollen, underground stems), and rhizomes (underground, rootlike stems). Like true bulbs, they look stunning in pots, though their flowering lasts only a few weeks. Still, the payoff is a bonanza and will tempt you to expand their numbers next year.

Of those that grow from corms, freesia, crocus, and dwarf gladiolus all make handsome pot plants. Plant several in a pot or bowl to grow in a sunny location.

Tuberous-rooted plants such as begonia, cyclamen, dahlia (shown here), and daylily grow large enough that just one plant easily fills a small pot. Tuberous begonia and cyclamen look best planted alone. Dahlias and daylilies associate well with other annuals and perennials in larger pots, as do ranunculus and harlequin flower.

Don't overlook plants such as agapanthus and dwarf canna that grow from fleshy rhizomes. Though clumps eventually become quite large, these plants thrive when their roots are crowded. You can leave them in the same container for many years. ✺

Colorful Summer Annuals

Although transient by their very nature, annuals offer quite an effect during a one-season lifetime. Vibrant pots of hot pinks, reds, and yellows cheer up edges of decks and patios along broad stretches of lawn. Cool blues and purples bring a quieter note to terra-cotta pots lining a brick entryway. However you combine and arrange them, containers brimming with annuals are guaranteed to please.

While their root systems remain small, annuals put the bulk of their energy into producing masses of blooms. In contrast to perennials, which endure winter's cold, summer annuals mature, blossom, and set seed over a period of just a few months; then, after a hard frost in autumn, they're gone.

To reap maximum bloom from summer annuals, it takes a bit of effort to pick off individual flowers just after they've peaked—a technique known as deadheading. This attention tricks the plants into producing another round of blossoms as they attempt to form seed.

Because their growth is so concentrated, annuals require regular feeding. For best results, mix in a slow-release fertilizer at planting or add a fractional dose of a water-soluble fertilizer every time you water. 🌸

COMBINING ANNUALS

Keep an eye out for pests on annuals, but use pesticides with restraint in outdoor living areas. Use plain water or soap sprays for soft-bodied insects, reapplying until the problem is solved. ✿

HAVE ON HAND:

- ▶ 14- to 18-inch square terra-cotta container
- ▶ Tub
- ▶ Potting mix
- ▶ Compost or peat moss
- ▶ Slow-release fertilizer
- ▶ Bark or moss mulch
- ▶ Scissors or pruning shears

Plants

- ▶ 3 dwarf zinnias
- ▶ 1 Baby Doll China pink
- ▶ 3–4 marigolds
- ▶ 3–4 sweet alyssum

Give plants a good soaking in their nursery pots. Allow them to drain thoroughly while you prepare the container.

Immerse a clean terra-cotta pot in a tub of warm water. Let container soak for about 30 minutes.

Fill the terra-cotta pot with a growing mix made of 2 parts soilless potting mix and 1 part compost or peat moss.

Plant dwarf zinnias in three corners of the pot, placing each plant near the edge of the pot.

Place multicolored Baby Doll China pinks in the fourth corner, and plant brightly colored marigolds in the center.

Fill any spaces at the edge of the container with sweet alyssum, allowing the stems to spill over the top.

HERE'S HOW

COORDINATING COLORS

Bright, colorful containers make a big impact on a garden scene. The key to their effectiveness lies in matching them with the hues and textures of your plants. Take blossom color into account when you choose a container for a group of flowering plants. Rather than clash or compete with vibrant blooms, the container should be neutral enough to underscore their appeal and temper any discord.

Water thoroughly. Cover the soil around plants with shredded bark or fibrous sphagnum moss to help retain moisture.

Remove faded blossoms to stimulate flowering. Plant several containers similarly, and group for best effect.

Alternatives

COTTAGE GARDEN FAVORITES

Favorite species of annuals that have withstood the test of time grow just as well in pots as they do in beds in front of a white picket fence. Part of their appeal is an old-fashioned sense of informality and charm as plants flop and intermingle. Position pots close together so stronger growers lend support to their neighbors, and be prepared for luxuriance and profusion as annuals hit their stride in midsummer.

Try to create balance in terms of height, but don't shy away from all the tall attractions. A pot of hollyhocks, bergamot, or love-lies-bleeding is indispensable surrounded by pots of lower growers such as dwarf China asters, long-blooming China pinks, and love in a mist. In a planter box, allow nicotiana to entwine its leafy stems through taller cosmos while petunias flow over the sides.

When designing your container garden, plan on grouping together those annuals with similar needs. Clarkia and sweet alyssum, for example, make a great team, are satisfied with low amounts of moisture, and bloom early, before intense summer heat begins. Later on, group impatiens and lobelia together in partial shade, but plant coleus separately so its strong branching trait doesn't overpower more delicate plants. 🌼

EASY-CARE PLANTS

Container gardening is never completely carefree, but you can minimize maintenance by planting annuals that thrive under tough conditions. When a heat wave hits at the height of summer, certain species stand up better than most and with less moisture. But because they are not completely drought tolerant, their potting mix should never go bone dry.

Common geraniums are one of the most adaptive plants for containers, not only for their brash color and bouncy shape but also for their willingness to take abuse and rebound with verve. Equally tolerant is dusty miller, grown largely for its silvery gray foliage that contrasts so soothingly with dark lilacs and blues. Try combining it with a purple trailing verbena, which also prefers somewhat dry conditions. Other easy-to-grow annuals are marigolds, lantana, snow on the mountain, California poppies, coreopsis, and blanket flower.

These easy-care plants all prefer fast-draining soil and a sunny site. They associate well together in small and large containers. For the most consistent bloom and best appearance over several months, mix a slow-release fertilizer into the potting mix at planting time and crowd plants close together. 🌼

Edible Gardens

Today's container gardens are no longer simply beautiful and functional. They're tasty, too. Bronze and purple-tinted lettuces, rainbow chard, red cabbage, yellow peppers, and other colorful crops rival flowering plants in their beauty, variety, and creative expression. Containers of edibles make themselves at home anywhere—on patios and decks, balconies and rooftops—allowing urban dwellers the satisfaction of growing some of their own food.

It makes little difference which crops you choose, since all vegetables and most fruits can prosper in containers. The best options, however, are dwarf or miniature, short-season varieties that are shallow-rooted. These require the least growing space. Lettuce and other leafy greens are the easiest to grow and the quickest to harvest.

Because most roots spread farther horizontally than vertically, wide planters 8 to 10 inches deep are the most versatile. But peppers, eggplant, melons, potatoes, squash, and tomatoes need at least 12 inches of soil or a 5-gallon container. Use a fast-draining potting mix; add slow-release fertilizer to maintain even moisture and a constant supply of nutrients. ❦

GROWING SWISS CHARD

Vegetables are never dull when you choose brightly hued varieties. Besides deep color, you'll also reap good nutrition and flavor. And don't be shy about showcasing edibles. In an attractive pot, they're even decorative enough for the front porch.

You can harvest chard for many months before it goes to seed. Even then, red-stemmed varieties look charming with sage and flowering plants, including red roses. 🌿

HAVE ON HAND:

- Seed-starter mix
- Seed trays
- Scissors
- 36 x 6-inch container
- Potting mix
- Slow-release fertilizer
- Pencil
- Additional 6- to 8-inch pots

- Pruning shears

Plants
- Seeds of Swiss chard 'Bright Lights'
- Red and green leaf lettuce
- Red orach or purple curly kale

Sow Swiss chard in seed trays filled with seed-starter mix. Use purchased trays with planting cells or clean, recycled containers.

Sow 2 or 3 seeds per cell. When the second pair of leaves appears, thin to 1 plant per cell by snipping stems at soil line with scissors.

Fill planting container with potting mix. Add an application of slow-release fertilizer on top of the mix.

Transplant when plants are about 3 to 5 inches tall. Start planting holes with a pencil, placing holes about 4 inches apart.

Transplant other colorful greens, such as red and green leaf lettuces, red orach, or purple curly kale, into other containers.

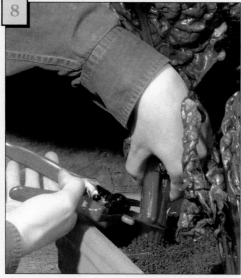

Arrange the containers in a sunny spot that is sheltered from the wind. Check the soil in the pots daily, and water when needed.

Use pruning shears to harvest tender young leaves, a few at a time, from the outside of plants. Leave enough foliage to keep plants looking full.

As plants get older, harvest entire plants by cutting them 1 to 2 inches above the soil. Plants that have been cut will regrow.

HERE'S HOW

STARTING FROM SEED

Planting seedlings from the local nursery is the fastest way to get a vegetable garden going, but your choices are greater when you plant your own seeds. Mail-order catalogs are more likely to carry varieties suited to container growing.

Package directions let you know when to start your seeds—usually a certain number of weeks before your last frost date. If you don't know the date for your location, ask at your local nursery or garden center.

To avoid fungal disease, always begin with fresh potting mix and clean containers. Most seeds germinate best in a warm spot where the temperature remains between 70° and 80°F. To help the soil stay moist, lightly cover the planting mix with clear plastic until sprouts appear. Then move seed trays to bright light until seedlings develop one or two sets of leaves and are ready for transplanting into their permanent container home.

Alternatives

TRELLISED VEGETABLES

Growing vegetables vertically is key to a bountiful harvest when gardening in containers. Within just a few square feet of container space, you can grow numerous vine crops by training them to grow on trellises, poles, or string.

Runner beans (shown here) and peas are routinely grown on supports in vegetable gardens of all types. The same technique works equally well in containers. A pole in the center of a pot or box with string anchored at the rim makes a perfect tepee for twining stems. Expect peas to reach about 4 feet high and pole beans a foot or more taller. Compact bush tomatoes, often called patio varieties, are popular for growing in pots; the most productive and best tasting grow tied to 6-foot stakes or within tall cages.

Members of the cucurbit family—squash, cucumber, and melon—actually have greater yields and superior fruits when trained vertically. On the ground, their fruits are subject to insect and disease problems, but suspended on a trellis, they hang gracefully, adding to the ornamental value of the garden. As they mature, tie up heavy squash and melons in fabric slings to prevent them from breaking off the vine before you're ready to harvest them. 🌿

FLAVORFUL FRUITS

Strawberries are so well loved that a container was created especially for them. A strawberry jar holds about a dozen plants in little pouchlike openings scattered around the sides. As a young plant matures and bears fruit, leaves and berries spill over the rims to bask in the sun. For a maximum number of berries, plant an everbearing variety that fruits all summer until frost. June bearers stop producing in early summer. Keep the soil moist, and fertilize regularly.

Managing trailing blackberry and raspberry brambles becomes complicated in containers, so they are best relegated to larger gardens. However, with pruning, both European grapes and rigid cane berries that you cut to the ground after bearing grow successfully in tubs that hold at least 5 gallons of potting mix. Because their roots are confined, the amount of fruit is limited, but you'll still have enough berries for breakfast and an afternoon snack.

Highbush blueberries are attractive ornamental, as well as fruit-bearing, shrubs. Just one is never enough, because blueberries bear the most fruit if you plant two different varieties. Plant each in a 5-gallon tub or larger, in humus-rich, acidic soil that stays constantly moist. 🌿

A Kitchen Herb Garden

Many cooks relish stepping to the kitchen door to cut fresh herbs. Growing them in containers ensures convenience and easy access when you place them near the doorstep. Herb gardens are ideal for a city garden growing in window boxes, as the small yield can be just the right amount you need for summer cooking.

Clay bowls and pots are classic herb planters, but don't let tradition limit your herb collection. You can create wonderful minigardens in hanging baskets, strawberry jars, and teapots. In large planters and boxes, there's no end to the possibilities. Many gardeners like to group containers of herbs together either for convenience or by theme, such as culinary, medicinal, or cosmetic herbs.

For a tidy design, it helps to plant herbs in identical or similar containers. For a more artful arrangement, group various pot sizes and perhaps a planted basket. There is no rule, however, about separating herbs from other plants. Many gardeners like to mix them with ornamentals. Mounding and trailing herbs such as parsley, sweet woodruff, chamomile, thyme, and sage lend a pleasing and aromatic touch to any container planting.

A STRAWBERRY JAR OF HERBS

The most important consideration in establishing a mixed herb planting is to group moisture lovers together and to plant Mediterranean herbs, which prefer drier conditions, separately. Sweet basil, chervil, coriander, and dill need constant moisture; rosemary, sage, tarragon, oregano, and thyme get by with less watering.

HAVE ON HAND:

▶ Strawberry jar, 30 inches tall

▶ Fast-draining potting mix

▶ Compost or peat moss mulch

▶ Liquid fertilizer

Plants

▶ Garden thyme, lemon thyme, or creeping savory

▶ Johnny-jump-ups or nasturtiums

▶ Oregano or Corsican mint

▶ Purple sage, sorrel, tarragon, chives, rosemary, or lavender

A strawberry jar makes a decorative and convenient container for growing herbs.

Fill to the first planting pockets with premoistened, fast-draining potting mix containing peat moss, compost, and perlite.

Remove enough herb transplants from growing packs to plant first layer. Good choices include garden and lemon thymes and creeping savory.

Position plants so foliage emerges from pocket and rootball lies on soil. Fill each pocket, then add potting mix to the next level.

Plant additional layers with edible flowers, such as nasturtiums and Johnny-jump-ups, or creeping herbs like oregano or Corsican mint.

Fill pot to about 2 inches from top with potting mix. Plant top layer with upright herbs such as purple sage, sorrel, tarragon, chives, rosemary, or lavender.

Water thoroughly. Cover soil surface with a thin layer of compost or fibrous sphagnum peat moss to conserve moisture.

Place container in bright or filtered light. Water when potting mix is dry 1 inch below surface. Apply half-strength liquid fertilizer every 2 weeks.

HERE'S HOW

GROWING HERBS IN POTS

Large herbs such as angelica, borage, anise, and fennel grow so tall and wide that they deserve to grow in their own pots. Their size may be intimidating, but each of these herbs adds a distinctive note that brings visual interest to any garden scene. Because all have taproots, they need pots at least 12 inches deep.

It's helpful to use a glazed pot for an herb garden, especially if you're unable to attend to it during the day. The glazing slows down water loss and keeps your herbs growing vigorously. But you must be careful not to overwater. If you use an unglazed pot in which water loss from soil will be greater, remember that drought-stressed herbs will stop producing the foliage you are trying to grow and instead will flower, then go to seed rather quickly.

Alternatives

EDIBLE FLOWERS

We usually think of vegetables first when planning an edible garden. But now that edible flowers have found their way into the kitchen, why not include them in containers along with other kitchen garden favorites? They'll enliven green and gray hues of vegetable foliage outdoors, and then complement a serving dish as a garnish.

Be sure to match edible flowers with their preferred growing conditions. In cool-season gardens, edge containers of lettuce, cabbage, and broccoli with pansies, violets, or calendulas. In warmer months, pair marigolds with eggplant, beans, and tomatoes. Edible fuchsia and tuberous begonia require shaded sites, while roses, daylilies, lavender, and bee balm do best in full sun.

In a few cases, you can harvest the flowers of a plant right along with its leaves or fruit. Squash blossoms still attached to the tips of newly formed squash make an appetizing display on a plate. Cut chive, cilantro, and mustard flowers with their greens for piquancy in salads and condiments. And, of course, you can perk up a planter box with nasturtiums' trailing stems and vibrant hues (shown here) and later perk up a salad with their spicy orange, red, and gold flowers. 🌿

HERB TOPIARY

Topiary art is commonly applied to formal, small-leafed shrubs for the landscape, but aromatic herb topiaries make a delightful container display in an herb garden. Woody-stemmed herbs such as rosemary, santolina, lavender, myrtle, and bay are excellent subjects. Each trimming releases wonderful scents and bits of herbs to use as you please. One or more balls on an upright stem are a classic outline, but you may prefer a spiral or other geometric form or decide to create your own fanciful silhouette.

To train an herb to a single stem, begin with a young plant that has a strong central leader (a single stem) with little branching. If the stem seems wobbly, secure it with a thin stake pushed to the bottom of the container. Use florist's tape and loosely tie the stem to the stake. As the plant grows, clip off side shoots and leaves from the lower half of the stem until the plant reaches two-thirds the height you want to achieve. At that point, pinch the top bud and allow a tuft of branches to form only at the top. Continued trimming will make the top fuller. If you want a series of vertical shapes, allow the central stem to grow taller until it reaches the height you like, then repeat the pinching and shaping. 🌿

Containers for Shade

Nearly every garden has some amount of shade for part of the day, but the source can vary considerably. Under open-branched deciduous trees, filtered or dappled shade is cast lighter in spring and heavier in summer, much as under a lattice-covered patio or arbor. Many plants thrive in these situations, and this is an ideal spot for containers, since they dry out more slowly than those in full sun. Watch for fluctuations of light, however, as shadows move away from pots of fuchsia, primroses, and other sensitive plants whose leaves may burn in direct sun. Be ready to move them to denser shade where light is bright but rays are indirect.

You'll want to take note of changes in the angle of the sun during the year to learn the extent that walls and fences obscure light. Watch to see if containers on the north side of a building or the inside corner of a porch receive any sun in summer, or if dense tree canopies allow enough light penetration for pots to be set underneath. Where sunless spots are bright enough, fill containers with shade-tolerant foliage of perennials, shrubs, and small trees. Reserve flowering annuals, perennials, and bulbs for light shade. ❧

SHADE-LOVING PLANTS

These shade lovers are versatile enough to thrive outdoors in mild seasons and indoors in winter. Though the container helps to restrict growth, you'll need to constantly pinch branch tips in spring and summer to maintain a balance of foliage on the coleus, flowering maple, and ivy. Don't hesitate to cut wayward branches on the flowering maple; it grows so rapidly that pruned growth will be replaced in no time. ❀

HAVE ON HAND:

▶ 18- to 24-inch-diameter pot

▶ Potting mix

▶ Mulch

▶ Pot feet

▶ Scissors

Plants

▶ 1 flowering maple

▶ 2 coleus

▶ 2 trailing begonias

▶ 2 spider plants

▶ 2 English ivy plants

Fill the container with moist potting mix to about 1 inch of rim. Gently tamp soil with fingertips to remove large air pockets.

With a trowel, make a hole toward the back of the container for the flowering maple. Loosen roots with fingers before planting.

Dig holes on either side of the flowering maple. Remove coleus from the nursery pots and set plants in place.

Plant 1 or 2 trailing begonias near front edge of pot. Set plants so stems and leaves drape over lip of container.

Plant a few small spider plants and specimens of English ivy close to begonias.

Use a gentle spray of water to settle soil after planting. Add a layer of decorative mulch to soil surface to conserve moisture.

Set plant beneath trees or in another cool, shady place. Put the pot on bricks or pot feet for good drainage and air circulation.

Pinch and trim coleus and ivy as needed to maintain compact forms. Using scissors, deadhead begonia blossoms to maintain vigorous flowering.

HERE'S HOW

PROMOTING LUSH GROWTH

Foliage on plants growing in shade begins to look sparse after a while unless you regularly apply fertilizer. But it must be added in small doses to avoid unsightly leaf burn and rampant growth. The safest approach is to mix in a slow-release product at potting time. When its potency is exhausted, mix in another application, or if your plants continue to thrive, you can wait until you repot to replenish the supply.

An alternative method is to fertilize with water-soluble crystals. Dilute to one-half the recommended dosage and apply twice as often.

Alternatives

WOODLAND BOUQUETS

While it may not be possible to transport a woodland into a small garden, you can certainly introduce the feeling of it into a shaded site. Begin with a boxed crabapple or Kousa dogwood and a trellised Virginia creeper. If space permits, add an enkianthus for its spectacular fall color as well as its lily-of-the-valley flowers in spring.

Each season, group different containerized wildflowers or your favorite shade-loving annuals and perennials under the boxed trees. In spring, blooming bulbs, forget-me-nots, and violets are indispensable woodland beauties. For a copious floral show, set out as many pots as you have room for. In a wide pot or tub planter, combine a bleeding heart, trillium, Virginia bluebell, and maidenhair fern. In summer, replace withered spring foliage with a mass of monkey flowers and pots of yellow and blue corydalis, foxgloves, New Guinea impatiens (shown here), and several late-blooming coral bells.

And plant a pot or two of alpine strawberries. As they mound up and bear bright red fruits for months on end, they'll satisfy with color, form, dependability, and, most of all, taste. Strawberries also work well as ground-cover edgings under boxed trees. ❦

FORMAL FOLIAGE

A covered entryway creates an immediate framework for a restrained collection of foliage plants in containers. In these somewhat formal areas dominated by shade, the greenery of potted shrubs and small trees invites visitors to stay and enjoy the restfulness and quiet dignity of the sheltered area.

Choices abound. Where winters are mild enough, the dramatic leathery foliage of camellia, skimmia, sarcococca, and David's viburnum stand in sharp silhouette year round. Where winter temperatures dip below freezing, you can maintain boxwood, holly, and yew in all four seasons. You might opt for a summer-only display with a fatsia or herbal topiary or the delicate foliage of a maidenhair fern (shown here). Pot your shade-loving selection in a container that emphasizes its formality, then add an equally disciplined trailing ground cover to underscore the shape and texture of the foliage. Variegated English ivy is perfect for its slow growth and shadowy highlights. Creeping fig offers small, shiny foliage that doesn't overcompete.

Fill two or three small containers to round out the display. A stiffly upright Myers asparagus fern; a pot of cyclamen, ranunculus, or violets; and a speckled pulmonaria nicely accent a foliage planting. ❦

Hanging a Wire Basket

Expanding upward is an efficient way to garden in a limited space, and planting in a wire basket is one of the most decorative. Unplanted, a wire basket looks a bit flimsy, but it is actually sturdy enough to hold considerable weight. Before making a basket selection, familiarize yourself with the various styles—aluminum, plastic-coated, and antique wrought iron—as well as lining materials. Sphagnum moss is perhaps the most attractive filler, but you can also use coconut fiber or pressed cardboard. Little of the basket or the liner will be visible after plants mature.

When planting in a basket, the most important considerations are weight and watering. Check the plant hanger and its attachment periodically for safety, and use the lightest possible potting mix, never soil. Always evaluate a watering method before you decide where to hang a basket. Keep in mind the need for frequent watering, since the potting mix dries out quickly when exposed to air. If you use a hose attachment, you'll never have to lift the basket up or down, but dripping is inevitable. Alternatively, an automated drip system waters when you're away, provides even moisture, and cuts down on messy spills. 🌸

CHOOSING THE PLANTS

Be sure to review the growth habits of the plants you select before placing them in a hanging basket. Here, the lobelia and sweet alyssum should be planted around the outside of a 12- to 18-inch basket because of their cascading habits. More upright growers like violas go in the upper half of the basket. Vertical plants like primroses, which do not drape at all, must be placed at the very top.

HAVE ON HAND:

- ▶ Tub of warm water
- ▶ Sphagnum moss
- ▶ 12- to 18-inch wire basket
- ▶ Lightweight potting mix
- ▶ Slow-release fertilizer
- ▶ Scissors and pruning shears

Plants

- ▶ 5–6 lobelias
- ▶ 5–6 sweet alyssum
- ▶ 3–4 geraniums
- ▶ 3–4 primroses

In a tub of warm water soak sphagnum moss until it is wet and soggy. Remove a handful at a time and squeeze out excess moisture.

Fill the spaces between the wires of a 12- to 18-inch basket with clumps of wet moss. Begin at the bottom and work your way to the rim.

Blend some slow-release fertilizer into a lightweight potting mix. Fill the basket to about an inch from the top, and water thoroughly.

Near the bottom poke a hole through moss with your fingers. Insert a transplant such as lobelia or sweet alyssum, rootball first.

Continue adding plants, poking holes and planting in an upward spiral pattern. Space the holes about 6 inches apart to allow growing room.

Plant the top of the basket with colorful, upright plants such as geraniums or primroses. Place the center plant first and work out toward the edge.

Use more sphagnum moss as a mulch to cover the soil surface. With scissors, trim away any unruly moss on the outside.

Hang the basket in a mostly sunny spot away from wind. Water well with a gentle hose spray. Deadhead plants to encourage flowering.

HERE'S HOW

GETTING STARTED

The easiest way to plant a wire basket is to fill it with 2-inch bedding plants. These have rootballs small enough to slip through the narrow spaces between wires. If your local garden center carries limited suitable varieties in 2-inch cell packs, you may need to start your own basket plants.

In fall, take cuttings from geraniums and licorice plants; make divisions of primroses or Italian bellflowers to over-winter and root indoors. Keep them in bright natural light or under a full spectrum fluorescent until you are ready to plant them. Start lobelia and sweet alyssum seeds indoors in February or early March for planting out in May. Try both the compact and the trailing varieties of lobelia for an interesting effect.

Alternatives

HUMMINGBIRD & BUTTERFLY BASKET

Few garden visitors are more welcome than hummingbirds and butterflies. You can lure these miniature aerial acrobats to your garden by planting hanging baskets of irresistible nectar plants. For an Oscar-winning performance, hang two baskets at some distance apart and watch hummingbirds dart between them and butterflies flutter gracefully along.

To attract the hummers, concentrate on red-toned, tubular blossoms that lack scent. Fuchsias alone are a powerful magnet, but you might like to add other species for a more intricate basket bouquet with both draping and upright plants. Nasturtiums, lobelia, and petunias are good choices for cascading types, while nicotianas, nemesias, annual salvias, and geraniums make good fillers.

For a more drought-tolerant hummingbird host, plant a basket of California fuchsia. Its lipstick-red, tubular blossoms offer delectable nectar.

To attract a succession of butterflies to your summer and fall garden, mix in some of their favorite plants with the hummingbird favorites or plant them separately. Lantana, verbena, scabiosa, monkey flowers, scented geraniums, and threadleaf tickseed continually entice with their repeat blooms over a period of several months. ❧

CASCADING BOUQUETS

Though long, dangling flower stems may be awkward in pots positioned on the ground, they don't have to be excluded from container gardens. They're perfect when suspended in wire baskets. In fact, lax stems are essential in hanging pots for their outward extension and graceful fall. If you hang your basket higher than 8 feet, plant an extra-long trailing species for a true vertical garden.

Verbena is one of the best trailing plants for a basket. It flowers in a wide range of colors, and its stems grow and blossom throughout the summer months into fall. Ivy geraniums and petunias (shown here) also bloom and trail in long streamers in a multitude of vivid hues.

For softer pinks, brighter corals, and wispier stems, plant diascia; for ever-growing lengths of yellow and gold, plant bidens and nasturtiums. In mild climates, try white, rose, or yellow African daisies for late winter and early spring bouquets. When planting a fuchsia, be sure to purchase a trailing type. Some varieties grow erect and are unsuitable for hanging containers.

And if floral balls and sprays don't appeal to you, experiment with cascading vegetables and strawberries for edible bouquets. ❧

Welcoming Autumn Flowers

For a fall composition of glistening color, start a container planting in midsummer with young plants not yet in bud. By the time autumn leaves are all ablaze, your container will be at its peak in full flower. All it takes is regular maintenance to carry seedlings through summer in top form. The payoff is a fresh burst of colorful blossoms for the end of the growing season.

Select flowers with hot colors for a vibrant display in a sunny spot. Pots of gold cosmos and blanket flowers, orange and red geum and salvias, and sunny sunflowers blend with deepening tones of early fall foliage. Single pots of chrysanthemums of any color are a must for fall. Before they form flowering buds, cut back their stems to keep them from growing overly tall. If they still need support, set thin stakes around the pot perimeter and loop twine or plastic all around. Mums tend to become unwieldy and flop over in wind and rain.

For a rainbow of bronze tints after an early frost, set out a pot of golden variegated Japanese forest grass. For rich contrast, pot purple pansies and a container of dwarf plumbago; its bright blue blossoms will contrast vividly with the reddish brown stems of the grass. ❦

CARING FOR FALL PLANTINGS

These autumn flowers need lots of sunshine. To keep them in full sun, you may need to move the pot as the autumn days shorten and the angle of the sun creates deeper shadows. Six hours of sun is the usual minimum for maintaining steady flowering.

HAVE ON HAND:

- ▶ Composted bark
- ▶ Peat moss
- ▶ Compost
- ▶ Perlite
- ▶ 14-inch-diameter terra-cotta pot
- ▶ Water-soluble fertilizer
- ▶ Green bamboo stakes
- ▶ Green florist's tape
- ▶ Spray bottle
- ▶ Chamomile tea

Plants

- ▶ 4–5 asters in 3- to 4-inch nursery pots

Purchase small plants of fall-blooming perennials, such as asters, in spring. Select healthy plants growing in 3- or 4-inch-wide containers.

Make a perennial potting mix by blending equal portions of composted bark, peat moss, compost, and perlite.

Fill an unglazed terra-cotta container to within 2 inches of the rim with moist potting mix. Tamp lightly and fill to the top.

Remove plants from nursery pots. Transplant to container, spaced about 3 inches apart around rim, with 2 or 3 in center.

Mix a supply of water-soluble fertilizer into your watering can. Water well. Repeat every 2 weeks.

Pinch back growing points when plants are about 4 inches tall. As new shoots develop, remove all but about 6 to 8 per plant.

HERE'S HOW

PROLONGING FALL COLOR

Just before a hard frost, cut the remaining blossoms and take them indoors to stretch out your enjoyment of their autumn colors.

If you plant strawflowers and want to dry them, cut the stems before the blossoms fully open. Then hang them upside down in tied bunches in a dry, well-ventilated place until completely dry.

As plants grow, set stakes into soil near stems. Every 6 inches along the stem, tie to stakes with green florist's tape.

Avoid powdery mildew by spraying foliage with cool chamomile tea once a week in late afternoon from midsummer.

Alternatives

JEWEL TONES OF AUTUMN

Expansive garden borders aren't the only place where you can stretch both the imagination and the bloom season. For the ambitious gardener, containers know no limits when summer's end draws near—not if you fill them with a new round of fall bloomers. Suddenly, you have new color and excitement, as though the growing season were just beginning.

Autumn hues rarely present themselves with the singular clarity that characterizes floral tones in spring. Lines between distinct shades blur as greens develop yellow and orangy hues. No plant group does this better than the grasses, which gleam in fall with metallic highlights. A clump of grass 2 feet tall or higher makes a dazzling centerpiece for a group of fall containers. Choose colors that complement the rich, jewel tones in the grass. A blazing red cardinal flower makes a gleaming accent against more subtle ruby reds, amethyst purples, sapphire blues, and deep golds of the grasses.

If you have a clematis vine, leave the platinum seed heads in place to sparkle in afternoon light. Plant autumn crocus and aconites to fill in under their leggy lower stems. Choose any of these late-blooming species to fill out your container display.

DAHLIA
Dahlia hybrids
1–5 feet tall
All zones
Red, pink, orange, yellow, purple, or white flowers; green or reddish to bronze leaves; many flower forms; standard potting mix; average water; full sun. Plant 4 inches deep. Dig for winter storage in zones colder than Zone 8.

GAZANIA
Gazania 'Daybreak Red Stripe'
6–10 inches tall
Zones 8–11
Wide, inviting daisylike flowers streaked with red; deadhead often to prolong flowering; well-drained potting mix with extra sand or perlite; water freely during growing season; full sun.

BLUE SALVIA
Salvia x *sylvestris* 'May Night'
18–24 inches tall
Zones 4–8
Violet-purple, upright flower spikes bloom from late spring to late summer; narrow green foliage; well-drained potting mix; low to average water; full sun. Great for regions with hot summers.

CHRYSANTHEMUM
Chrysanthemum 'Vampire'
18–24 inches tall
Zones 5–9
Abundant rich red flowers on strong stems in late summer to fall; attractive dark green leaves; standard potting mix; average water; full sun; excellent cut flower; for best bloom pinch growing tips two or three times in spring.

LOBELIA
Lobelia erinus 'Sapphire'
3–6 inches tall
All zones
Many small, deep bright blue flowers with a small white throat all summer; bronzy green mounding foliage; humus-rich potting mix; average water; full sun. Tender perennial grown as annual to mound over edges of pots, perennial borders, footpaths, and driveways.

An Evergreen Planting for Winter

Green is a valuable commodity in winter scenes. An evergreen conifer (a cone-bearing shrub or tree) in a container qualifies as a special prize when all else appears bleak against gray skies, a snowy backdrop, or dull vegetation. Because its branches are usually stiff and formal, a conifer works best as a single planting in a container rather than combined with other plants. Arrange it where it best enhances your landscape, either as a focal point or as a background element for smaller pots.

Look closely at its form before you purchase a conifer and consider whether it will outgrow the setting you have in mind. Rather than try to reshape one that may not respond, it's better to shop for a different plant. Most conifers need little pruning and do best when allowed to develop their natural form.

Choose a container spacious enough to accommodate the root system but not so large that soil will remain soggy after watering. Roots are able to take up only a limited amount of moisture at a time.

For winter, be sure your planting zone is suitable for overwintering trees in pots. You may need to move your tree indoors for the cold season, or at least protect it against the cold with extra mulch or a polyester row cover. ❧

WINTER CARE FOR CONTAINER TREES

Wherever hard freezes occur, containerized trees can experience root damage and desiccated foliage. Check the soil in winter to be sure that it contains some moisture, even when frozen. Insulate the pot to prevent alternate freezing and thawing, which heaves roots above the soil. If possible, move the container to a sheltered location during the most severe winter weather. In very cold climates, choose an alpine variety of spruce, pine, or fir that is hardy in your zone. ❧

HAVE ON HAND:

▶ 12- to 24-inch stone container

▶ Topsoil

▶ Potting mix

▶ Hand fork

▶ Pruning shears

▶ Scouring brush

▶ Bubble wrap

Plants

▶ 3-foot-tall Hinoki false cypress

Measure the nursery container to determine the size of the rootball. Select a new container 2 to 4 inches wider and deeper than the rootball.

Combine 1 part topsoil with 3 parts potting mix. Partially fill container with potting mix so conifer sits at same depth as in nursery pot.

Loosen soil from top of rootball and fill in all around. Water as you work to settle the soil. Smooth a thin layer of soil on top.

Maintain an evergreen's shape by pruning branch tips in spring when new, pale green growth appears. Thin out crowded branches.

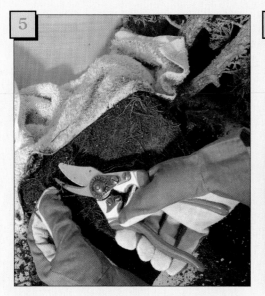

Every 1 to 2 years lift and inspect the rootball. Brush away soil on the outside and prune any wrapped and crowded roots.

Clean the container and scrape off any accumulated salt deposits. Add fresh potting mix under and around the rootball as you repot.

In summer protect the evergreen from hot, drying winds and reflected heat. Water frequently and hose off accumulated dust.

In winter protect from wind and severe cold using bubble wrap. Decorate the branches with strings of popcorn and cranberries for the birds.

HERE'S HOW

SELECTING A CONIFER

Conifer choices vary widely. Not all, of course, are available at local nurseries and garden centers, but specialty growers stock unusual varieties. If you're looking for something statuesque, don't settle for a common juniper or arborvitae. Look instead for a variety of these plants that has been developed to grow in the shape you need, or go further afield and choose a false cypress cultivar, a Japanese cryptomeria, or other interesting specimen that's hardy in your area.

Alternatives

WINTER SILHOUETTES

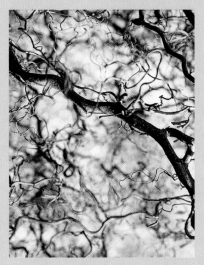

In the winter bare branches often reveal shapes that lie hidden under cloaks of foliage in other seasons. While some species offer little appeal in their deciduous states, others take the spotlight. It's the smart container gardener who chooses trees and shrubs with multiple seasons of interest. Happily, there is a good selection that performs well in box planters as long as you provide a porous potting mix and good drainage. If you live in an area where winter temperatures drop below 10°F, you'll need to move your container plant to a spot where temperatures remain near freezing.

The twisted branches of a hazel known as Harry Lauder's walking stick (shown here) become increasingly gnarled and sculpted as it ages; in winter it's a star attraction. Somewhat more treelike, crape myrtle offers a more subtle architectural appeal: Outer grayish brown bark on its muscular trunks and branches peels off to reveal pink-hued inner patches. The cultivar 'Fantasy' has more striking reddish brown bark. Many Japanese maples are exquisite in their leafless form. The mahogany bark of the paperbark maple curls and peels off in thin strips. A bit rougher but ruggedly handsome, oakleaf hydrangea also sheds cinnamon-colored bark all winter long. ❦

WINTER BERRIES

Dull, bare branches will come to life in winter when filled with clusters of showy berries. Winterberry holly (shown here) stands in sharp relief whether you leave it as a spreading shrub or train it to tree form. Choose among red-, orange-, or yellow-fruited cultivars—red is best to attract birds. The berries are restricted to female plants, but you need a male plant nearby for pollination. A nice combination of deciduous hollies suitable for containers is the female variety 'Sparkleberry' and its male counterpart 'Apollo'.

Rose hips in myriad hues and beautyberries in lilac tones also paint charming pictures in winter. Many rugosa roses bear very attractive fruits, but their shrubby habits are difficult to maintain in a pot. Some roses, such as redleaf rose, offer red stems and fruits that last all winter long. Some barberries, cotoneasters, and viburnums also hold berries over winter.

In mild climates berries cling to several evergreen shrubs for many months. Mahonia assumes a striking upright form with stiff, spiny leaves and bluish purple berries. Try it in a glazed pot near an entry. In full sun firethorn and heavenly bamboo brandish clusters of bright red fruits within their green foliage. ❦

Year-Round Containers

Many gardeners depend on containers for all their gardening. Poor soil conditions or limited space may be the reason, but there are other motives, too. Containers make it easy to take your garden with you when you move. And many gardeners use them to experiment with new species or to dabble with color schemes before planting permanently in the ground. If a new plant doesn't work well in one position, simply try it in another. Moving a container into a garden bed or changing locations to an entryway quickly gives a whole new perspective. A Japanese maple ablaze with fall color may be just the answer to fill a corner of the patio with festive autumn décor while the same tree spends the rest of the year in a border.

Projects in this section show you how to make continuous use of containers. You'll see how some trees and shrubs do best as a single specimen, but others partner harmoniously with different plants. Larger containers welcome the addition of cascading ground cover, the bright blooms of flowering plants, or a blend of foliar grays and greens.

You may want to reserve a few containers for perennials with seasonal interest. As one plant nears the end of its show, move it aside until it shines again. Or freshen your design with a parade of perennials as each comes into its prime. By choosing species that thrive in your climate, you'll be proud of your container garden year round. ❧

Seasonal Replacements

Picture-perfect containers inevitably feature plants at the top of their performance, never during their decline. If you've wondered how to maintain such ongoing perfection, try the project here to prolong months of bloom in a single container. The secret lies in a twofold approach. The first step is to cut back selected plants after their first round of flowering, reducing their size so they reshape themselves for rebloom in a later season. The second step is to remove annuals as flowering wanes and swiftly replace them with plants just coming into bloom.

The trick is balance and timing. Throughout the year, choose a blend of plants that complement each other at all stages of their growth, and never allow a plant to remain past its peak. Of course, this means that you must anticipate a plant's decline by noticing when flower buds stop forming and foliage begins to brown. Be on the lookout for changes in your plants as you make your rounds watering and grooming. And have well-developed replacements just coming into bloom on hand and ready to go. By watering and fertilizing regularly, you will maintain an uninterrupted flow of blossoms for many months. 🌸

MAINTAINING A LONG SEASON OF BLOOM

To avoid time-consuming maintenance over several seasons, look for shortcuts in caring for containers. Rain and cool weather lessen demand for frequent watering in spring, but dry spells later on call for daily watering. During warm weather use an automatic irrigation system, or place containers where a lawn sprinkler delivers a light spray. ❧

HAVE ON HAND:

- ▶ 18 x 24-inch tub planter
- ▶ Potting mix
- ▶ Slow-release fertilizer
- ▶ Wire hoops and row cover

Plants

- ▶ 2–3 tuberous begonias
- ▶ 3–4 petunias
- ▶ 4–6 ivy

- ▶ 4–6 impatiens
- ▶ 2–3 pentas
- ▶ 2–3 dwarf nicotiana
- ▶ 2–3 daisies
- ▶ 2–3 heliotrope
- ▶ 4–6 scaevola
- ▶ 4–6 coleus
- ▶ 4–6 pansies
- ▶ 4–6 sweet alyssum

Select a container about 18 x 24 inches. Provide drainage holes in the bottom, and fill with potting mix; add slow-release fertilizer to the mix.

In spring plant some tuberous begonias in the center and surround with assorted petunias.

Set ivy plants along edge of container with stems draping over the side. Fill remaining area with white and pink impatiens.

In early summer add heat-loving flowers. Replace begonias with brightly colored pentas and dwarf nicotiana.

Surround pentas and nicotiana with daisies and blue and white heliotrope. Replace ivy with rich blue scaevola.

In late summer replace pentas and nicotiana with coleus. Pinch off new coleus buds to encourage bushy growth.

Add cool-weather plants such as pansies and white and blue alyssum along the outside of the container.

To extend bloom time if frost is expected, insert wire hoops into soil and drape heavyweight fabric row cover over hoops.

HERE'S HOW
CREATIVE CONTAINERS

Choose a container that holds your interest throughout the year, since your multiseason potted garden will be on display for many months. For a rustic or antique look, choose a discarded wheelbarrow or a wagon. You may be lucky enough to find an old iron or copper pot. If you prefer a more modern expression, try clustering three or four sections of galvanized or clay drainpipes at staggered heights in place of a single container.

Remember that plants depend on fast drainage. If you settle on a drainless container, consider planting in a plastic or fiberglass pot that will be set inside the drainless container so that you can pour off excess water.

Alternatives

A PERENNIAL GARDEN

Growing perennials where brick and concrete are more prominent than garden soil takes a bit of effort but never fails to improve your landscape. You can go all out and grow potted plants that peak every few weeks, or you can take a less rigorous approach and strive for simplicity.

By focusing on just a few perennials, as was done with the hostas shown here, you can still create vivid impressions of color and variety, especially if you select distinctive plants. For example, a large-leaved hosta, such as blue-gray 'Elegans' or variegated 'Northern Exposure', looks best without a surrounding bevy of miscellaneous pots. But at the same time such an eye-catcher does well in the company of one or two alluring bloomers.

In spring set out single pots of a short-season performer such as aubretia, basket of gold, or evergreen candytuft. Later on, rotate in veronicas and lilies or bellflowers and hydrangeas as each comes in and goes out of bloom. When the hosta is dormant, alter the scene with pots of snowdrops, heath, or winter-blooming iris. If you need to fill in with more height, consider a trellised vine or a hanging basket.

SUMMER-LONG BLOOMERS

Annuals satisfy our desire for summer color with their exceptionally long periods of bloom. No other group of plants can fill their role. If you're looking for fast, imposing height along with summer-long blossoming, choose spidery cleomes or tall nicotianas. For low, spreading annuals that trail, try 'Classic' zinnia, multicolored moss rose, or bright-eyed morning glories. To attract hummingbirds, choose rich red snapdragons, salvias, and zinnias. Plant sweet alyssum, marigolds, cosmos, and verbena to lure butterflies.

Geraniums and petunias are two of the most valued summer annuals for their exuberant color and ability to withstand high heat. For exquisitely frilly blooms, choose Martha Washington geraniums and ruffled petunias. Include trailing ivy geraniums and double-flowered grandiflora petunias in a hanging basket.

Plan to spend a little time every few days grooming your potted annuals. While some, such as impatiens and ivy geraniums, self-clean their spent blooms, most annuals do not. Their repeat flowering is most dependable when you deadhead. As fast as you snip off faded flowers, the plants will form new buds in a continuous stream.

Enjoying Trees in Pots

Visual balance in any garden calls for movement in every direction. Adding a tree to a grouping of container plants achieves this effect by lifting the eye up and over potted plants that mound and sprawl. A tree also influences the fall of light over nearby foliage, creating interesting patterns of valuable shade and casting fleeting shadows and sunny highlights throughout the day.

Although your available space determines what type of tree you might add to your garden, keep in mind that height and a broad canopy call for a large container and a considerable volume of soil. Nearly any small tree will survive for several years in a pot no larger than 10 gallons, but it will remain dwarfed as long as its roots are constricted.

In making your selection, consider whether the tree's rate of growth and seasonal appearance are compatible with its growing site. Determine whether it will reside permanently in the same place or whether you will have to relocate or repot it frequently. If you grow a larger tree in a 24-inch box, it will be difficult to move but roomy enough for roots to develop. Wood planters are sturdy enough to withstand winter's stress and also provide stability in wind.

POTTING A JAPANESE MAPLE

B efore you begin, decide whether your boxed tree will be a permanent fixture or whether you will be moving it around. A box in a fixed spot is a good idea if your soil conditions are unsuitable for growing. But if you intend to move the container, be sure to settle on a manageable size. 🌼

HAVE ON HAND:

▶ 18- to 24-inch wooden planter box

▶ Nontoxic wood sealant

▶ Potting mix

▶ Topsoil

▶ Compost or composted bark

▶ Pruning shears

▶ Slow-release fertilizer

▶ Sphagnum moss or bark chip mulch; marble chips (optional)

▶ Bricks

▶ 4 plastic trash bags of leaves

Plants

▶ 3-foot-tall Japanese maple

Select a sturdy wooden container slightly larger than the plant's rootball. Seal the planter box inside and out with nontoxic wood sealant.

Prepare a humus-rich, soil-based mix by blending 2 parts potting mix with 1 part topsoil and 1 part compost or composted bark.

Fill the container with enough soil so the top of the rootball will be 2 inches below the rim. Remove the plant from the nursery container.

Free large roots from side of rootball and trim with pruning shears if needed. Center plant in the container. Make sure the trunk is straight.

Fill remainder of container with potting mix. Gently firm soil around edges of the rootball. Sprinkle some slow-release fertilizer on the mix.

Cover the soil surface with sphagnum moss or decorative bark chips. If pets trouble your plants, use a layer of marble chips to discourage them.

Move the tree to the spot where it will grow. Set the container on bricks or other support for good drainage. Water gently until thoroughly moist.

In cold climates prepare your plant for winter by filling plastic bags with leaves in the fall. Place bags around the pot.

HERE'S HOW

JAPANESE MAPLE CARE

Japanese maples are available in dozens of cultivars. Make your selection based on the role it will play in your landscape and your preference for leaf size and color.

Most cultivars are multitrunked and low branching. They tend to develop their own unique form, which can be damaged by careless pruning. As you maintain your tree, prune only as needed and always with an eye to preserving the natural shape.

The most critical maintenance step for your Japanese maple in a container is watering. The soil must never dry out more than 1 inch below the surface, but neither should it become soggy. Hot summer weather poses the greatest risk. Try this approach: If the temperature stays below 90°F, plan to water every third day. When the mercury moves above 90°F, check daily, but plan to water every other day.

Alternatives

PATIO TREES

Small-scale trees can contribute substance and décor to all container gardens, whether they are on a patio or deck, in a courtyard, or on a rooftop. Many gardeners like to move their potted trees indoors into a bright space for half of the year and then back outdoors during mild weather.

Most specimens are selected for a particular attribute. While deciduous species are common in northern climates, evergreens as well as palms and treelike bamboo are popular in mild regions. Broadleaf evergreens like privet, sweet bay, and citrus are easily clipped into geometric shapes to control their size, but these must be sheltered from harsh winter temperatures. Flowering redbud, plum, cherry, crabapple, Carolina silverbell, Korean dogwood, fringe tree, deciduous magnolias, and weeping pear are all more adaptable to a broader range of climatic conditions. Though they may remain in place during winter if you plant them in boxes, it is beneficial to line containers before planting and to wrap them with several layers of insulating materials to prevent containers from breaking and to avoid alternate freezing and thawing of the rootball. ❦

CONIFERS

Conifers are successful long-term container trees when they are well nourished and watered. But in pots, evergreens are rarely able to recover from severe drought stress. They respond more agreeably than most other trees, however, to having their roots confined in pots, allowing you to select nearly any of the myriad varieties. Though a 24-inch box is needed for a tree to reach more than 8 to 10 feet of height, it's possible to plant conifers in smaller pots. Dwarf varieties are naturally inclined to restrict their growth, and there are hundreds to choose from, though you may have to contact a specialty grower to find a specific cultivar.

Consider the many forms that conifers assume and the different appearances of needles before you make your choice. Most share the advantages of the delicate texture of their foliage and the well-behaved form of their stiff branches. The classic cone is just one among weeping, twisted, and globe shapes. Some false cypresses, podocarpus, Norfolk Island pine, and redwood flourish in most southern zones. Yews, junipers, pines, umbrella pine, firs, spruces, and weeping Atlas cedar (shown here) withstand the rigors of colder climates. ❦

Growing an Evergreen Shrub

An evergreen shrub in full flower assumes a role of authority among pots of herbaceous annuals and perennials. This is the time to rearrange the other containers, letting them defer to the seasonal splendor of the shrub's blossoms. But as the flowers fade, move the shrub to the background, and let the other plants take over. In the end, such an evergreen may actually be more valuable to a garden scene as a supporting player than as a star.

If you choose an evergreen foliage plant with small leaves that look attractive when clipped, its role changes when you reshape it. Pruned into a spiral tower or compact globe, it becomes rather formal and quite elegant year round. Boxwood is the classic choice for this kind of shearing. It has a different purpose in your garden than a less formal flowering shrub. Containers of sheared boxwood make effective accents nearly anywhere, typically in pairs framing an entry or flanking a walkway. You can use them as a framework for an herb garden or to define a sitting area. Some of these evergreens look best with an underplanting of trailing English or ground ivy or a flowering creeper such as 'Snowflake' water hyssop. 🐾

GROWING A SHADY EVERGREEN

An evergreen foliage plant will grow in a more shaded site than a flowering plant, but it still needs bright light for part of the day. Check the growing requirements carefully if you plan to put your plant in a dim courtyard, under stairs, or in any other enclosed location. In very low light, foliage stays healthiest if you rotate the plant with another in a brighter spot so that both get adequate exposure to sun. 🌱

HAVE ON HAND:

- ▶ 14- to 18-inch terra-cotta pot
- ▶ Tub of water
- ▶ Compost
- ▶ Perlite
- ▶ Aged bark
- ▶ Potting mix
- ▶ Pruning shears
- ▶ Mulch
- ▶ Hedge shears

Plants

- ▶ 24-inch-tall rounded boxwood

Select a terra-cotta container that is 2 inches wider and deeper than the rootball. Soak in a tub of water until thoroughly wet.

Combine 1 part each compost, perlite, and aged bark and 2 parts potting mix for a fast-draining, lightweight medium.

Remove boxwood plant from nursery container. Use pruning shears to trim away any coiled roots from the rootball.

Fill the container with a few inches of potting mix. Set the plant in the container and fill with mix, tamping lightly as you work.

Cover the soil with a 1- to 2-inch layer of mulch, such as bark chips or buckwheat hulls. Leave air space around trunk of plant. Water well.

To avoid leaf damage from sun and drought, set plants in partial shade, and water when top 1 inch of soil is dry.

Whenever growth appears ragged, use hedge shears to clip naturally rounded plants into round shapes and conical ones into cones.

Rejuvenate older plants in spring. Use hedge shears or pruning shears to remove one-third of growth. Fertilize.

HERE'S HOW

CONTROLLING GROWTH

Developing plants need to be moved into larger pots each year to give their roots room to grow. At some point, though, you can leave the plant in the same size container, depending on the amount of top growth you want to allow. By restricting the roots, you'll also curb top growth. To keep your plant vigorous and healthy, inspect the rootball annually and prune crowded roots as needed to prevent them from becoming wrapped or bound.

Alternatives

EVERGREENS FOR CONTAINERS

Evergreen shrubs are some of the most rewarding and versatile container plants. In pots they never become an overgrown thicket or brushy wood as they sometimes do in the ground. Instead, the restraint a container exerts on their roots keeps them in bounds so that you can use them as valuable screens and accents.

For many evergreens, foliage is the outstanding ornamental feature, while for others it is their flowers. It's a tough decision which to choose when space is at a premium. Happily, there are plenty of handsome evergreens that not only flower, though briefly, but also bring graceful foliage to a small garden year round. In tight spaces choose a shrub with an upright branching form rather than one that forms a mound or spreads freely.

In some situations you'll want to place a line of containerized shrubs for privacy or as a windbreak to simulate a hedgerow. If you decide to leave the plants in place permanently, you can even clip them. You can shear pittosporum, boxwood, and various conifers into formal shapes or leave them informal and unsheared. 🌸

GARDENIA
Gardenia augusta
6 feet tall or more
Zones 8–11
Antique white flowers with many thick-textured, gracefully curved petals; blossoms intensely perfumed; leaves shiny green; well-drained, humus-rich potting mix; moderate water; shade.

JAPANESE UMBRELLA PINE
Sciadopitys verticilatta
20–25 feet tall
Zones 5–9
Tapered spire of glossy evergreen foliage; needles arranged like spokes on a wheel; slow growing; well-drained, acidic potting mix supplemented with bark and sand or perlite; keep moist; partial shade. Needles may turn bronze in winter.

MOUNTAIN LAUREL
Kalmia latifolia 'Bullseye'
6–10 feet tall
Zones 5–9
A dense, bushy shrub with oval-shaped, glossy, dark green leaves. Large clusters, 3 to 4 inches across, of cup-shaped white flowers, heavily banded red-purple within. Moist, fertile, acidic potting mix in partial shade or in sun where mix remains moist.

HOLLY
Ilex 'China Girl'
10 feet tall
Zones 5–8
Hybrid female holly with glossy, dark green leaves; bears large clusters of deep red fruit in fall; humus-rich, acidic potting mix made with bark; full sun to shade; keep moist. Plant male variety such as 'China Boy' nearby to produce fruit.

RHODODENDRON
Rhododendron 'Anna H. Hall'
6 feet tall
Zones 5–8
Evergreen shrub with large oval leaves. Bears trusses of open funnel-shaped, white flowers, 2 inches across, with intense pink buds; fast-draining, humus-rich, acidic potting mix; water frequently; morning sun or shade.

Planting a Bonsai

Limitations of space are usually seen as a liability when it comes to any kind of gardening, but not for someone who takes up the ancient art of bonsai. By drawing on inspiration from nature, you can create miniature landscapes in only a shallow tray. Whether you build an entire collection of conifers, deciduous trees, flowering shrubs, and ground covers or simply introduce a single bonsai into your container garden, it will add a distinctive flavor. No other potted plant is so specialized.

A bonsai lets you visualize the broader strokes of a landscape on a small canvas. By intricately training a conifer or other type of plant, you can make it appear to stand on a windswept bluff, a craggy mountain, or even in a grove of trees.

This living sculpture remains a dwarf as long as you restrict its roots in a small container. Its beauty deepens over many weeks and years as you continue to imitate the forces of nature by pinching and pruning to produce contortions that, in the end, appear to be quite natural.

Try to display your bonsai against a plain background to show off its sculptural lines. Like most other trees, it thrives only out-of-doors. You can take it inside, but keep it there no longer than a few days. 🌿

AN EVERGREEN BONSAI

Once you become adept at creating bonsai, you'll want to train a young seedling, but to begin, choose a plant that is already well developed. Give frequent attention to its growth and care, mainly to develop a pleasing outline and to prevent the small container from drying out. Lift out your bonsai every year at first, then every other year to trim roots and repot. ❧

HAVE ON HAND:

▶ Manicure scissors
▶ Copper wire
▶ Pruning shears
▶ Potting mix
▶ Bonsai growing container
▶ Water-soluble fertilizer

Plants

▶ Juniper suitable for bonsai

Select a juniper or similar shrub in a small pot. Look for uneven branching with foliage rising from the top of the branches.

Use scissors to prune out all but one vertical stem. Thin remaining growth and remove all shoots and leaves on undersides of branches.

Shorten any long branches and wrap them loosely with wire, leaving ends loose at the trunk. Remove plant from nursery container.

Cut away lower half of rootball with pruning shears. Use fingers to loosen roots and soil around rootball.

Add potting mix to bottom of growing container. Set plant slightly off-center in pot. Finish adding soil, then water.

Bend the wire ends near the trunk and push them into the soil. Bend the branches gently to the desired shape.

Keep plant shaded for 1 week, then move to full or partial sun. When possible water with rainwater. Avoid using chemically softened water.

Wait 3 months after potting to fertilize with water-soluble fertilizer every 3 to 4 weeks from early spring to fall, except during heat spells.

HERE'S HOW

CARING FOR A BONSAI

Fit wires on young, flexible branches, but use caution when you bend them to shape. It takes many months for replacements to grow. Leave wires in place no longer than 6 months, to avoid scarring.

Pinching new growth is important for achieving the desired shape and forcing leaves to grow close together. In summer you may want to trim any large leaves on established trees to give the plant more of a dwarf appearance.

Though your bonsai will rest in winter, keep its roots slightly moist and protected from severe frost and freezing temperatures.

Alternatives

A FLOWERING BONSAI

Many bonsai plants require patience and years of training before assuming a satisfying shape. With a flowering bonsai, your efforts are rewarded with annual blooms while the tree grows into a living sculpture.

Few flowering shrubs are more impressive in bloom than the azalea (shown here). Of the hundreds of cultivars, the dwarf Satsuki and Kurume hybrids are most often used for bonsai. The Kurumes develop a tiered structure—a highly prized bonsai form.

Quince and crabapple are also popular bonsai plants because of their beautiful bark, spring flowers, summer fruits, and fall color. Another good choice is firethorn, which holds clusters of red berries into winter. For unusual silvery flowers, fruits, and foliage, try silverberry.

Perhaps the fastest growing bonsai is bougainvillea. Although it demands constant pruning, it also blooms nearly continuously, most heavily in spring. Wisteria is also vigorous, though its long, drooping blossoms appear only in spring. Serissa, a prolific summer bloomer, is a favorite because of its tiny single or double blossoms and very small leaves. All these blooming plants need repotting and root trimming when flowering is finished. ❧

A BONSAI WITH AUTUMN COLOR

One of the joys of bonsai gardening is watching a deciduous tree brandish dynamic colors as it changes with the seasons. Some favorite trees for bonsai include beech (shown here), ginkgo, larch, sweetgum, and oaks. Among the maples, the trident maple is popular for its small leaves and gnarly roots, but the Amur maple is a better choice for cold climates because it stands up to frost.

Roots grow very quickly on young bonsai trees, so be sure to trim them as you repot before buds open in spring. Older trees need repotting only every two to three years. Wait until summer to fertilize after repotting; otherwise, feed trees once a month from spring to autumn with a slow-acting, balanced fertilizer or every other week with a half-strength liquid solution. Prune branches at the same time as you prune the roots to avoid overstressing the root system. Then as your tree grows, shape it by pinching back branches to the first or second set of leaves. Thin, new shoots will be more in scale with the miniature tree. If a vigorous, older tree is not going to be repotted, remove up to one-half of its leaves every other year in early summer to produce a new, smaller set. ❧

Quick and Easy Topiary

The art of manipulating trees and shrubs to create a garden topiary requires a trained eye and skilled hand, as well as a great deal of attentive shearing. A faster way to achieve a pleasing geometric or fanciful shape is to train flexible stems over a wire frame. This quick method, called false topiary, leads to finished results in just a few months instead of years.

Vines and creepers make a fast go of it, but various thin-stemmed shrubs and ground covers work, too. You can make your own frame or purchase one in nearly any shape. Preformed birds, butterflies, and even teddy bears add a fanciful presence when placed in containers and covered with green.

Because topiaries themselves are the focal point, plant them in plain rather than highly decorative containers; simple terra cotta is usually just right. Take note of the size of the wire frame you intend to use and choose a container that fits the scale of the frame. English ivy and creeping fig are two of the easiest plants to work with. Baby's tears and thyme-leaf fuchsia, as well as winter creeper, jasmine, and honeysuckle, may also be used. ❧

AN IVY TOPIARY

U se a simple wire frame to train a topiary or fill a sculpted frame with sphagnum moss. A textured, porous filling gives the ivy something to cling to. Growth is fastest when you mist the moss frequently to keep it damp. If you can't find a hollow frame or ready-made enameled wire frame to purchase, bend heavy-duty wire into a circle or any other shape you'd like, leaving an end at the bottom long enough to press deep into the pot for support. 🌿

HAVE ON HAND:

▶ 18- to 24-inch-diameter urn

▶ Potting mix

▶ Wire topiary frame

▶ Green florist's tape or florist's wire

▶ Horticultural scissors

▶ Spray bottle

▶ Pesticidal soap

Plants

▶ English ivy in a 6-inch pot or larger

Fill 18- to 24-inch-diameter urn to about 1 inch from top with moist potting mix. Gently firm mix with your hands. Add more as soil settles.

Form a hole in the center slightly larger than the plant's rootball. Plant the vine, spreading stems so they radiate around the pot.

Insert a sturdy enameled wire frame into the rootball to act as a permanent support.

One by one, wind each trailing stem around the frame. Use green florist's tape or florist's wire to secure the tip of each stem to the frame.

For thick, even coverage, alternate between winding stems clockwise and counterclockwise over wires. Overlap as many stems as possible.

You can either trim back side shoots to encourage fuller growth or allow some to grow out and tie them to the frame.

Set the topiary out of direct sun but in a bright location. Mist the foliage frequently, but water only when surface of soil is dry.

Periodically check beneath the leaves for spider mites. If you find mites, spray plant with pesticidal soap per label directions.

HERE'S HOW

MAKE YOUR OWN FRAMES

Topiary sculpture becomes doubly creative when you make your own supporting frame. Choose any shape that suits both your fancy and the container. For a three-dimensional look, weave together pliable willow or birch to hold ivy stems. Geometric shapes are easiest, but anything goes, from dolphins to rabbits to people. Be sure to anchor your frame solidly in the pot. A thin metal rod or length of bamboo works well. For larger frames, use two or three anchors.

Get a head start on success with a wire frame by beginning with good-quality material. Choose enamel-coated or copper-coated steel wire of a low enough gauge to be self-supporting. Try to avoid taking too many shortcuts as you bend it to shape. Angles can be bent fairly accurately using your fingers or a pair of needle-nose pliers, but rely on a fixed support to form curves. A tin can, post, or pipe is perfect for making circles and arches.

Alternatives

A FORMAL CITRUS TREE

Oranges and lemons are some of the most delightful plants to grow in a container. Not only is the fruit decorative as it develops, but for much of the year the tree is bedecked with lightly scented blossoms. Though citrus trees must have winter protection in most climate zones, they grow very well in containers small enough to move without too much trouble. You can keep a young tree in a 5-gallon pot for one or two years, but beyond that, it's wise to repot in a barrel tub or box at least 18 inches wide and 12 to 18 inches deep.

If you allow citrus to grow naturally, the structure of its branches will be open and airy, but if you regularly prune it to train it into a small, compact tree, you create what's called a "standard." You may be lucky and find a citrus already trained as a standard when you buy it. If not, start with a young, single-stemmed tree and remove its side branches until the trunk reaches the desired height, usually 3 to 4 feet.

In any case, always buy a dwarf variety for container culture, ideally a tangerine or mandarin orange, the most cold-hardy types. Other possibilities are calamondin, dwarf lemon, dwarf lime, limequat, and kumquat. ❦

A ROSE STANDARD

Sometimes called tree roses, rose standards evoke idyllic, old-fashioned scenes with their rounded, blooming heads. They look best planted with a companion ground cover around the base.

Rather than try to train a rose to grow vertically, purchase a plant that has been grafted onto a suitable trunk and rootstock—ask for advice where you buy the plant. Even though the stem appears sturdy, bolster it with a stake (a metal rod works well) that runs from the full depth of the container into the branches.

A standard requires the same regular watering and feeding as any rose for good health and continuous flowering. And like other rose forms, it needs careful pruning to stimulate new growth and flowering. With a standard, however, you'll be pruning to create a symmetrical dome shape as well as to renew flowering wood. The usual recommendation is to prune just enough to maintain an attractive shape during the growing season, then remove about one-half of the head during dormancy so that the branches are 8 to 12 inches in length. If you notice any shoots developing along the stem or above the graft, remove them immediately. ❦

Focal Points

Transforming a collection of container plants into an organized garden takes a bit of doing. It helps to have a plan from the very beginning, but if you don't, you'll need to periodically reexamine what you've got. Look carefully at the mix of shapes, growing patterns, foliage, and flowers that you've gathered, and note strengths that call for emphasis and weaknesses to be disguised. Perhaps a rampant grower is overstepping its bounds and obscuring its partners, or the partners are too restrained to be included at all. Ask yourself if anything stands out as notable or if you can perceive a unifying element among your various containers. If not, you may need to introduce a focal point to organize your design and how it is viewed. You'll want to accentuate the strong points not only of your plant collection but also of the space where it resides. The best way to do this is with a striking specimen plant or a unique group in one container.

The projects in this section will help you find a focal point. There are examples of exotic tropicals and succulents, plants with forceful sculptural lines, and color-packed arrangements. Each of them immediately calls for recognition and stands out as a star attraction. As you make a selection, have in mind how it will blend into your garden and what else the eye will see when it is drawn to the new focal point. Then arrange your containers around it to show them off to best advantage. ❧

A Dramatic Planting

Oversize stems and leaves—those with sharp outlines and an architectural form—rival works of art. They stand out in any situation, calling for all eyes to look their way. In a container, a bold plant becomes an instant focal point that you can feature as an island in a landscape, a filler in a long formal flower border or shrub bed, or a highlight near a pool. Use such plantings at transition points in the garden—to mark corners and divisions between garden rooms, for instance. In small gardens, a spectacular foliage plant accompanied by other plants with complementary textures and colors immediately creates an imposing accent in an entry area or courtyard.

When you feature a dramatic planting, pay as much attention to the container as to the plants. Ordinary terra cotta is never wrong, but consider glazed clay, faux stone, fiberglass, and cast iron as other more interesting materials.

Choose from plants running the gamut from shrub and tree standards to opulent tropicals to attention-getting succulents and cacti. Giant-flowering annuals, perennials, and grasses, as well as specialty conifers, also deserve to take the spotlight. 🌸

EYE-CATCHING FOLIAGE

This planting is best for warm climates. Cold snaps may damage foliage, but the plants will not be seriously harmed. Pale blue accents combine well here with vibrant reds, but you can substitute bronze or purple tones if they blend better with your garden scheme. 🌿

HAVE ON HAND:

- Half-barrel planter
- Perlite
- Topsoil or compost
- Potting mix
- Slow-release fertilizer
- Mulch
- Water-soluble fertilizer

Plants
- 1 bird of paradise
- 1–2 angelica
- 1 blue oat grass
- 3–4 dahlias
- 3–4 dusty miller
- 2–3 sedum 'Autumn Joy'
- 1–2 ivy

Select a container that accents this dramatic mix of plants. It should be about twice as wide as the rootball of the largest plant.

Combine 1 part perlite, 1 part topsoil or compost, and 3 parts potting mix. Add slow-release fertilizer, moisten lightly, then mix thoroughly.

Fill container with potting mix. Remove bird of paradise from nursery pot and set in back-center of container.

Add more potting mix to the container and place the angelica next to the bird of paradise. Add blue oat grass.

Fill in with more potting mix as you work. Plant smaller flowering and foliage plants, including dahlias, dusty miller, and sedum 'Autumn Joy'.

Plant the trailing plants, including ivy, around the edges of the container, where they can hang over the lip of the pot as they grow.

Water well with tepid water to settle the potting mix. Add a layer of mulch, such as bark chips, to the container, and water again.

Once a month during the growing season fertilize the planting with a complete water-soluble fertilizer. Mix the fertilizer per label directions.

HERE'S HOW

DECORATIVE MULCHES

Water loss from evaporation is one of the chief maintenance concerns in container gardens. You can take steps to forestall moisture loss by covering the soil surface with a mulch. Under a dramatic star attraction, you'll want to choose a complementary decorative material such as shredded bark, bark nuggets, or small river stones. All are good looking and easy to find.

Use a living mulch that requires little moisture itself. A low-growing ground cover such as moss, sedum, thyme, or snow-in-summer works well with nearly any kind of plant. But you may want to customize your planting. For instance, if you are featuring a bold burgundy canna with bright blossoms, plant a zonal geranium or coleus that mirrors its colors. Under dark green foliage, plant English ivy with a cream variegation.

Alternatives

IMPRESSIVE PERENNIALS

Not all gardens or gardeners are amenable to architectural specimens, but even though their period of bloom isn't long lasting, stately perennials are too appealing to resist. While many perennials are compact and rounded or trailing in form, there are many that grow tall in a single season or two. Foxglove and some bellflowers, for example, form basal rosettes their first year, and the second year give rise to elegant flowering stalks. Such plants deserve particular attention and should be planted in their own containers. Where there is room to grow them, the same applies to delphinium (shown here), lily, melianthus, ligularia, and rodgersia. A tall but slim *Verbena bonariensis,* in contrast, works better as a wispy companion, slipping through loose branches of bushier plants.

If you are tempted to plant a gargantuan gunnera, Chinese rhubarb, or umbrella plant, be prepared in advance. Though all are exquisite, they need soil that is constantly moist to succeed. Do this by mixing plenty of moisture-retentive polymers into the potting mix and lining the container with a heavy-duty plastic bag to eliminate drainage. ❧

GIANT GRASSES

Ornamental grasses make impressive container plants in several ways. Distinctive in form and character, some appear as upright bundles while others arch and sway freely with the slightest breeze, often whispering as they move. Bronze autumn colors pale to straw in winter but lose no glamour under a sprinkling of snow. It's only when they are cut to low mounds before spring that they relinquish their role as stars in containers. Tender species aren't in view during this downtime, since they must be sheltered over winter.

The giant grasses—such as pampas grass, maiden grass, silver grass (shown here), purple moor grass, fountain grass, and feather grass—quickly grow large and have special needs if you want to keep them in prime condition. Most of all, they want constant moisture and regular feeding to satisfy their densely fibrous root systems. Lacking regular care, grasses won't reach their potential size. They should never be exposed to drought conditions, which cause foliage to die back, detracting from their appearance. Well-tended grasses are among the most striking of all container plants and are worth the extra effort it takes to maintain them. ❧

Tropical Designs

Tropical plants, long popular as houseplants, are enjoying a revival in the garden. By growing tender species in pots in northerly climates, you can give them the special treatment they require to survive outdoors for many years. The number-one concern is protection against cold: frost in spring and fall and low nighttime temperatures anytime. Moisture and exposure are other key issues. Plants native to tropical rain forests thrive only when they're kept constantly moist and surrounded by high humidity. Some must have full or partial shade and will not tolerate direct sun, or their leaves will burn. And most, especially large-leafed specimens, do not withstand strong wind.

Bulbs and bulblike plants like canna, calla lilies, and watsonia are the easiest tropicals to grow in containers because they die to the ground each year, so they can be lifted from pots and stored. When growing tender climbers, such as bougainvillea, jasmine, mandevilla, and passionflower, provide a trellis or other support directly in the container. This allows you to move the plant under shelter at a moment's notice.

Vines prefer smallish pots relative to their size. A larger container results in excess foliage and fewer flowers. ❦

TROPICAL MANDEVILLA

Mandevilla's twining stems want to carry it to 20-foot heights or more, but in a container this vine looks best climbing over a short trellis, a rounded frame, or a stout stake. Flowering is heavy from spring until fall, as long as you provide adequate nutrients. You'll notice a drop-off in blossoming once the fertilizer runs low. Keep nitrogen to a minimum, however, or you'll get a lot of foliage with few flowers. ❧

HAVE ON HAND:

▶ Compost

▶ Potting mix

▶ Perlite

▶ 18- to 24-inch planter box

▶ Hand fork

▶ Trellis

▶ Slow-release fertilizer

▶ Green florist's tape or twist ties

▶ Pruning shears

Plants

▶ 1 mandevilla in a 10- to 12-inch pot

Mix equal quantities of compost and a soilless potting mix; blend in a handful of perlite. Fill an 18- to 24-inch square pot half full with mixture.

Loosen roots around the outside of the rootball. Set rootball in container so that the top is 1 inch below the container rim.

Fill container to within 1 to 2 inches of the top with additional potting mix. Push trellis into the rootball near the existing support.

Water to help settle soil. Fertilize with a balanced, slow-release product such as 14-14-14.

Tie stems to the trellis with loose loops of florist's tape or garden twist ties. Check every 2 weeks and tie new growth as needed.

Set the pot where it will be sheltered from wind and midday sun. After a few weeks, original support may be removed, if desired.

HERE'S HOW

GARDEN TROPICALS

Containers present the perfect solution to growing tropical plants in the garden alongside hardy perennials. Simply sink a tender tropical in a clay or plastic pot into a garden bed to enjoy its exotic flowers and foliage throughout the summer. Before night temperatures drop to the mid-40s in autumn, lift the pot and cut back the foliage, then winter your plant indoors. Just as buds swell and growth resumes in spring, trim roots, repot in fresh soil, and fertilize lightly to ready your plant for another season of tropical splendor in the garden.

In late fall when flowering slows, cut back vines by one-fourth and side shoots to 3 buds each. In winter keep at 55° to 65°F; water sparingly.

When new growth appears in late winter, begin watering more generously. In spring lift rootball, trim any coiled or damaged roots, and repot.

Alternatives

TENDER PERENNIALS

Some of the most beautiful species of plants have their origins in tropical or subtropical climes. While many of the sages, for example, are hardy in the temperate zones, dozens are too tender for planting in many gardens; yet you can enjoy quite a few of these if you grow them in containers. One of the most rewarding is autumn sage, which blooms for long periods from early summer on, despite its name. This small-leafed, woody perennial grows in a loose mound and flowers profusely. As days shorten and temperatures dip in autumn, blossoming slows. Before the first hard frost, cut the plant back and move its container to a protected spot where temperatures are just above freezing.

Other tropicals are flashier and more suggestive of an exotic origin. Several ginger lily species, for instance, produce spikes of delicate, porcelain-like flowers on reedy stems with large, smooth leaves. Ferns and orchids of all types, a multitude of South African daisies, plumbago, and glory bower are just some of the tropical delights to enjoy in warm seasons. Besides warmth and moisture, they depend on regular fertilizing and fairly large containers for healthy root growth. ❦

TENDER TREES

Size alone makes it hard to protect tropical trees in cold climates. But there are several that are relatively easy to manage. Angel's trumpet (shown here) grows so rapidly that you can cut it to within 6 inches of the ground and it will grow 4 to 6 feet in one year. Trained as a standard, its foliage spreads wide and it bears highly scented, dangling, trumpet-shaped flowers. During winter storage, keep soil barely moist. Discard trimmings, as all plant parts are toxic, and avoid growing entirely if young children or pets are present.

Just as angel's trumpet is impressive for its fragrance and flowers, banana dazzles with its magnificent foliage. Long leaves cluster at the base then extend outward, flopping in great arches. The most dynamic foliage is tinted red or purple; edible fruits are secondary. If frost damages a banana plant, it will regrow from the roots in spring.

Most other showy tropical foliage that you grow in containers must be moved indoors to bright light during cold weather. Tree ferns, palms, cordyline, and dracaena stay small enough to double as houseplants for many years. Some flowering trees such as plumeria and citrus also continue to flourish during several months indoors. ❦

A Focus on Color

A sure way to attract attention is to brandish bright colors. Gleaming reds and yellows stand out, while pale creams and pinks are more reserved, and deep greens recede into the background. But intensity isn't the only way to create a focal point in a garden. Harmonizing hues of any color catch the eye and draw it in for more intimate observation. It is this overall pleasing effect of blended tones that invites the garden visitor to come closer and linger.

In a container garden, color plays a special role. Just as variations in a single petal meld together to give the impression of one hue, combinations in one container fuse into a balanced whole. You'll want to test out shades of a single color before you plant to determine how well they combine. Be prepared to make adjustments as you group colors. Perception changes under varying light intensities at different times of the day, and colors may appear different at home than they did in the nursery.

In year-round container gardens, pay closest attention to leaf color. Flowers come and go, but foliage remains. ❀

A HOT-COLOR PLANTING

If you start from seed, buy color-labeled packets so you end up with the tones you want. Purchase transplants after buds have opened so you know what colors you're working with. Try various shades of yellow to separate disparate colors, but use white sparingly and only as an accent. Don't hesitate to try unusual groupings; bold colors attract the most attention. ❦

HAVE ON HAND:

- 18-inch-diameter terra-cotta pot
- Peat moss
- Perlite
- Compost
- Mulch
- Water-soluble fertilizer
- Pruning shears

Plants

- 1 banana plant or bird of paradise
- 1 flowering maple
- 1–2 nasturtiums
- 2 marigolds (Marietta hybrids)
- 2 licorice plants
- 1–2 tassel flowers
- 1–2 lantana

Fill container to about 2 inches from the top with potting mix made of equal parts peat moss, perlite, and compost.

Dig a hole and transplant a tall, large-foliaged plant, such as banana or bird of paradise, at the back of the container.

In the center of the container plant a flowering maple. Be sure to set the plant so that its stem is straight.

In front of the flowering maple plant 1 or 2 nasturtiums. Set plants so the trailing stems fall over the edge of the pot.

On either side of the tall, large-foliaged plant, set some brightly colored marigolds, such as Marietta hybrids.

Plant licorice plants next to marigolds. For the best display, tip rootballs slightly away from the edge of the pot.

Fill out the container with tassel flower and lantana. Add a layer of mulch, such as cocoa hulls, to keep soil moist.

Fertilize every month with a balanced water-soluble fertilizer such as 20-20-20. Deadhead flowers regularly.

HERE'S HOW

UNIFYING WITH COLOR

Color is just one of many ways to organize a group of container plants, but in the end, it is perhaps the most satisfying. It is on this basis that many plants make their way into our gardens in the first place. The perfect arrangement of colors gives structure and unity to an individual container, as well as to a garden as a whole.

Consider the entire container grouping when you're planning a color scheme so that you can balance the effects of flowers, plant shapes, and foliage. Place intense color combinations, as well as white flowers, in the background, where they will seem to emerge and appear closer. Place dark blues and purples up front, or they may fade in the distance and be lost. Use paler tones in shaded sites, which cause them to appear brighter than they do in sunlight. Brilliant red, orange, and even white are best in sunny sites, which wash out some of the intensity.

Alternatives

MOOD COLORS

Various people react differently to single-hued blue, pink, and yellow color schemes in a garden. Soft blues and lilacs tend to soothe and inspire peacefulness. Red, in contrast, is irrepressible and universally acknowledged as lively and compelling. A little red that echoes burgundy stems or bronze foliage is charming, but too much red overpowers. The challenge, then, is to balance containers with the right quantity and tone of any color. A red with a touch of yellow may appear orange, while red with blue will look rosy, and the orange and rose hues may be incompatible. It helps to select your container plants in bloom so you end up with what you are expecting. Remember, too, that reds will leap forward, making them perfect in one setting but too jarring in another.

Bright colors can be quite effective as a single accent in a container, especially when you are dealing primarily with foliage. In this situation, just a few vivid and long-blooming gerbera daisies can be a perfect touch, whereas in masses they could be overwhelming. 🌸

SIBERIAN IRIS
Iris siberica **'Soft Blue'**
24–30 inches tall
Zones 3–8
Strong stems in late spring; narrow, grassy leaves are strongly upright in habit; well-drained potting mix; keep soil moist; full sun to light shade.

DALMATIAN BELLFLOWER
Campanula portenschlagiana **'Resholt'**
6–8 inches tall
Zones 5–7
Large clusters of erect, open, bell-shaped violet-blue flowers from late spring to summer; often reblooms in fall; dense mats of heart-shaped leaves good for spilling over edges of pots; standard potting mix; average water; partial shade. Fast-growing perennial.

PRINCESS FLOWER
Tibouchina urvilleana
3–10 feet tall
All zones
Tropical shrub from South America with satiny gray-green leaves; from spring to fall bears cup-shaped royal blue flowers; average potting mix; average water; full sun with light midday shade; prune to shape in late winter.

CLEMATIS
Clematis x jackmanii
5–20 feet tall
Zones 5–9
Large bluish purple flowers on new wood in summer; dark green divided leaves; soil-based potting mix; average water; full sun/afternoon shade. Can be cut to the ground; vines grow fast in one season; twisting, curling stems cling to supports.

SPEEDWELL
Veronica **'Waterperry Blue'**
6–12 inches tall
Zones 4–8
Dainty spreading perennial with medium green leaves; spikes of light blue flowers held above foliage in spring; well-drained potting mix; average water; full sun to partial shade.

Dry-Climate Gardens

Desert plants and succulents are most at home in arid climates, but in containers, they can be grown nearly anywhere. They're among the most easy-to-care-for plants, which partly explains their popularity, but they have much more going for them besides low maintenance. Cacti and succulents have some of the most intriguing forms of all plants, and this increases their value as focal points in a garden.

Whether you choose the perfect, deep burgundy rosettes of a branching aeonium or the unfolding spirals of a turquoise and yellow agave, a container of succulents provides subtle fascination. Jade plants offer a spectacular haze of pale blossoms, and the rich reds, oranges, and yellows of kalanchoe, sedum, and echeveria flowers stand in lovely contrast to their thickened, tinted foliage.

Because many succulents and cacti are small plants, it's tempting to make a grouping of many small pots and add to it to create the effect of a special collection. Prize specimens deserve their own containers, but you'll cut down on clutter by planting many of the more common plants in one pot. The garden here is a good example of how to economize on space by planting many varieties in one large, shallow container.

A DESERT GARDEN

Shallow containers with drainage holes and gritty, fast-draining soil are both key to maintaining an arid garden. These conditions provide the fast drainage succulents and cacti need to keep roots from rotting. The greatest threat from excess moisture comes in late fall through winter, when plants are dormant. During active growth, though, succulents need frequent watering.

HAVE ON HAND:

▶ Sharp sand or perlite

▶ Peat moss

▶ Vermiculite

▶ 36-inch-square shallow container

▶ Gloves

▶ Pruning shears

▶ Slow-release fertilizer

▶ Fine gravel

Plants

▶ 1 yucca

▶ 2–4 echeverias

▶ 1–3 jade plants

▶ 5–6 hens and chicks

Evenly blend a fast-draining potting mix made of equal parts sharp sand or perlite, peat moss, and vermiculite.

Mix in water until evenly moist. Add mix to within 2 inches of rim of a shallow 36-inch-square container. Tamp lightly with fingers.

Prune long roots of yucca and plant near center. Set the echeverias in clusters around container at the same level they grew in nursery pots.

Plant jade plants and hens and chicks near the echeveria. Set hens and chicks at a slight angle so rosettes show well.

Add slow-release fertilizer per label instructions; avoid getting pellets on foliage.

With a narrow trowel, carefully sprinkle a layer of small stones over soil. You can add driftwood or colorful stones as accents.

Water this dry-climate planting only when soil is nearly dry, and then soak soil thoroughly. Overwatering encourages disease.

Remove dead blossoms with pruning shears or scissors, cutting stalks as close to rosettes as possible. Remove leaf litter regularly.

HERE'S HOW

MANAGING A COLLECTION

Once you begin gardening in containers, it's always tempting to add just one more pot, especially when potting small, low-maintenance succulents and cacti. As your collection grows over the months or years, step back and take an overview. Try to be objective in assessing the growing assortment of pots by keeping an eye on aesthetics and weeding out the poor performers. Observe your plants one by one and consider whether they could be more attractively displayed by grouping several in a single pot or by regrouping the pots themselves. If you spread them out on a porch, for instance, you might want to rearrange them on a display rack with two or three levels of shelves.

Alternatives

SHAPELY SUCCULENTS

Of the many features offered by cacti and succulents, shape is the most alluring. Perfectly rounded globes, towering spires, and rosette clumps are the most typical, but there are many other unusual forms. Some species are as small and smooth as stones or form ground-hugging, bumpy mats. Still others develop a tall stem and then branch like a tree.

When planting these unusual succulents in a container, consider their rate of growth, mature size, and ease of handling. Many species can remain for years in the same container, but a barrel cactus, for example, becomes increasingly fatter and eventually must be repotted into a larger pot. Unless you're prepared for sticky business, you may want to grow less prickly types. Consider also where you will place the containers. Arid gardens must be viewed up close to be appreciated, but if you grow plants with sharp spines, you may want to keep them at a distance.

Cacti are the most well-known succulents, but there are many other species that store water in thickened stems and leaves. Aloes, kalanchoes, lithops, many euphorbias, and—surprisingly—a few geraniums are succulents that make excellent container plants.

KALANCHOE
Kalanchoe blossfeldiana
1 foot tall
Zones 10–11
Clusters of red, pink, orange, yellow, or white flowers on slender stalks in spring and summer; succulent, glossy green, notched leaves; humus-rich potting mix; low to moderate water; fertilize monthly during growing season; partial shade.

PINCUSHION CACTUS
Mammillaria spp.
2–12 inches tall
Zones 9–11
Spiny sphere or cylinder forms spreading clumps; small flowers usually yellow, white, pink, or red; some hairy species have whitish appearance; fast-draining, gritty potting mix; low water and humidity; full sun. Increase water and fertilizer in spring.

DRAGON BONES
Euphorbia lactea
2–4 feet tall
Zones 10–11
Easy-to-grow succulent with long candelabra-like stems of mottled green with prominent thorns; fast-draining, gritty potting mix with plenty of sand and perlite; water sparingly; full sun.

GOLDEN BARREL CACTUS
Echinocactus grusonii
6–24 inches tall
Zones 10–11
Warm-climate plant with rows of golden spines covering round, dark green, fleshy stem; showy, bright yellow flowers in summer; fast-draining, gritty potting mix; full sun; low water. Water and fertilize in spring for profuse blooming.

ALOE
Aloe vera
12–18 inches tall
Zones 10–11
Evergreen, tender perennial with rosette of swordlike, fleshy leaves spotted with gray; sandy, well-drained potting mix; average to low water; full sun to light shade; sap traditionally used to treat minor burns.

Roses in the Landscape

Whether in pots or in the ground, roses never fail to draw attention. Their rich blossoms stand out as focal points, yet they combine beautifully with a multitude of other plants. If you have highly alkaline and sandy soil or heavy clay and poor drainage, you may have a struggle growing roses. But you can pot your roses so that you can enjoy them in containers throughout the landscape. You can be adventuresome and grow the rambling or climbing rose you've always admired. Support canes on a south or east wall, or train them on a fence or trellis. If you don't have a fixed support, you can still provide height and vertical interest by adding a sturdy trellis to the container itself at planting time and then letting the potting mix hold it firmly in place.

Even where garden soil presents no particular problem, growing a few roses in containers lets you put them in beds and borders without fear that companions in the ground will outcompete them for moisture and nutrients. You also have the option of wheeling a perfect polyantha rose or a brilliant floribunda rose into the spotlight just as it reaches its full glory. Then set it aside until it is at its peak once again.

A POTTED ROSE

For a true focal point, choose an everblooming rose, such as a floribunda, rather than one that blossoms only once in the early season, such as a gallica. With good maintenance, regular water, and fertilizer, a container rose will flower continuously from spring through fall. ❧

HAVE ON HAND:

▶ 12- to 24-inch stone planter

▶ Perlite

▶ Compost

▶ Peat moss

▶ Gloves

▶ Fertilizer

▶ Posts/trellis

▶ Green florist's tape

▶ Pruning shears

▶ Evergreen boughs

Plants

▶ 1 English climbing rose in a 10- to 12-inch pot

Measure equal parts perlite, compost, and peat moss. Combine ingredients, moisten, and blend until uniform.

For container-grown roses: Remove plant from nursery pot. Add a layer of soil to container, insert plant, and fill with soil.

For bare-root roses: Fill pot halfway with a mound of soil. Place plant roots over mound. Fill with soil and firm gently.

Fertilize immediately after planting and then monthly with a commercial rose fertilizer. Move container to growing location.

Set support posts or trellis about 1 foot from container. Use green florist's tape to tie canes, or stems, to support in a fan pattern.

Deadhead spent flowers as needed. Use pruning shears to cut just above the second leaf below the faded blossom.

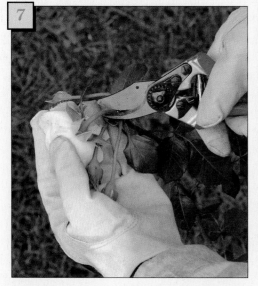

For both repeat- and once-blooming varieties, prune side shoots to 4 buds after each flush of bloom.

In cold climates sink container to rim in loose soil in late fall. Water thoroughly; mound evergreen boughs over plant.

HERE'S HOW

WINTER CARE OF ROSES

During winter dormancy prune canes of most roses by one-third to one-half. More drastic pruning delays spring bloom and reduces the number of flowers, though it does result in larger roses. Miniatures need little pruning, but you should cut out all deadwood. On climbers, remove the oldest one or two canes after the third year to encourage new growth.

While roses are dormant they require little water, but the soil in the container should never become bone dry. Provide just enough moisture to prevent both the roots and the canes from dehydrating. If you store containers in an unheated garage or outdoor shed in a cold climate, be sure to mound soil and leaves over the crown just as you would if your roses were in the ground.

Alternatives

ROSE ACCENTS

For many rose lovers, the hybrid tea is queen of the garden and the rose of choice. This sensitive hybrid is a demanding plant to use in containers, yet its beauty may be well worth the effort it requires. But other roses also supply classic blooms and are superior in specific situations. Ground-cover types become beautiful accents as they cascade over the edges of planter boxes under large shrubs and trees; you can use miniature forms in pots with annuals and perennials. Compact polyantha roses are perfect container accents, providing instant color in outdoor living areas as well as in the garden. They're small enough to be easily portable, and they make great fillers for bare spots in beds and borders.

Plant roses in a porous terra-cotta or wood container to allow for air movement, but use a plastic or fiberglass pot for less weight and greater ensurance against moisture loss. Mature miniatures, polyanthas, and small floribundas must have a 12- to 14-inch pot, while larger types need even more room to spread their roots. Small containers are suitable only for very young plants. Whichever container you choose, never allow the potting mix to dry out. A 2-inch layer of organic mulch helps to conserve moisture. ❧

PRIZE ROSE

Your favorite rose deserves a place of honor in the garden. You can highlight an individual shrub by singling it out for container planting and placing it where it stands in contrast to its surroundings. Move a highly scented rose into the foreground around a patio table or near an entry, but set a prickly specimen where people won't accidentally brush against it. To emphasize pastel blossoms, set your container against a darker backdrop such as a hedge or stone wall, or even on steps where it marks a change in elevation.

To maintain the health of your prize rose, note the advantages and limitations of your growing site. In humid climates place containers where there is ample air circulation. In more difficult dry regions provide steady irrigation and protect foliage and roots from intense afternoon sun and drying winds. Adding extra compost should help to retain moisture and preserve some humidity around the plant as well. In any situation avoid too much shade; roses need at least six hours of sun a day for best bloom. Although they must be in sun, try to provide a degree of shade in front of the pot to protect roots from overheating. In northern zones move the container indoors in winter to avoid cold damage. ❧

Ornamental Grasses

Ornamental grasses change in character throughout the year, but they always command attention. Whether they appear as mounding clumps of wispy foliage in spring, bedecked with feathery flowers in summer, golden and glowing in autumn, or dusted with snow in winter, they never fail to please. Many tall grasses emerge as living sculpture when they reach their full height, while others nestle in small hummocks.

When you select a single grass for your container garden, decide which time of year you'll most count on this as a feature. The purplish pink to creamy white flower heads of fountain grass, for example, are most pleasing in summer. Switch grass, feather grass, and tufted hair grass are also striking specimens in bloom, and become more attractive as the seed heads and leaves turn bronze in autumn.

Of the hundreds of choices, nearly all can be grown in containers, but it is most convenient to limit your selection to small or medium-sized grasses. In all but the mildest climates, you may want to narrow the field further to tender and annual species and sidestep the chore of providing protection in cold weather. Then, as your grass begins to disintegrate in winter, merely discard it. ❧

POTTING GRASSES

If any of your grasses grow so rapidly that they force soil out of the pot, lift out the rootball and then repot the plant in a larger container.

When dense tufts make it difficult to water from the top, set pots in a saucer and add water from below. Empty any water that is not absorbed after an hour; use a kitchen baster to remove water from under pots too heavy to lift. 🌿

HAVE ON HAND:

- ▶ 12-inch pot
- ▶ Peat moss
- ▶ Perlite
- ▶ Compost
- ▶ Shredded bark
- ▶ Pruning shears
- ▶ Mulch
- ▶ Wooden plant label
- ▶ Evergreen boughs or leaves

Plants

- ▶ 1 fountain grass
- ▶ 3–4 vinca or ivy

Select container and fill halfway with potting mix made of peat moss, perlite, compost, and shredded bark.

Remove fountain grass from nursery container. Use pruning shears to trim away thick or matted roots on rootball.

Set plant in pot, adding or removing soil so top of rootball is about 2 inches below rim.

Use a thin-bladed trowel to transplant trailing plants, such as vinca or ivy, along edge of container.

Space trailing plants every 4 inches around pot.
Add a layer of mulch to within ½ inch of rim.

To check soil moisture, insert a clean wooden
plant label into soil. Wait a minute and with-
draw. Water plant if label is dry.

HERE'S HOW

VERSATILE GRASSES

Plant a collection of grasses in individual pots with good drainage.

Plant all grasses in a water-retentive,
soil-based growing medium.

If you have a large clump of grasses, move it into a larger pot.

In cold areas overwinter outdoors by tipping
container on side. Remove vinca. Completely
cover with evergreen boughs or fallen leaves.

Before new growth begins in the spring, cut back
the old growth 6 to 8 inches above the crown
with pruning shears.

Alternatives

GRASSES IN COMBINATION

The fine lines of grass foliage lend a unique texture to a grouping of potted annuals and perennials. Grasses can be included in the same pot with blooming broad-leafed plants, or you may prefer to pot them separately.

With the wide variety of colors and sizes of grasses, you won't have any difficulty finding the right one for any color combination or seasonal display. In a grouping of spring wildflowers or bulbs, for instance, include a low sheep's fescue or blue oat grass, both of which also bloom in late spring. Northern sea oat is a perfect plant during hot summers; in either full sun or partial shade, its rich green foliage has a cooling effect that tones down bright pinks and reds. In autumn, feature the nodding spikelets of quaking grass for a graceful addition to pots of black-eyed Susans and purple salvias.

To illuminate a shaded corner of a water garden, submerge pots of a variegated grassy-leafed sweet flag and umbrella plant to reflect light mirrored from the water's surface. Around the water's edge, group pots of variegated iris, white-blooming nicotiana, and the tall silver grass called 'Morning Light' (shown here) to further brighten the spot.

SMALL GRASSES

Small grasses are by far the easiest to manage in a container garden. They require less work to trim, divide, and pot, and they combine well with many other plants throughout the entire growing season. It's easy to move these pots from one seasonal grouping to another, providing you with an instant new garden. Plant several small containers, so you don't have to limit yourself to just one type of grass. Numerous species, such as fescue (shown here), produce miniature forms that adapt readily to growing in pots.

The fescues are best known and widely available. They grow in neat, tight clumps of blue, silver blue, blue-green, or bright green. Their fine flower spikes appear to sit on oversized pincushions, or you can trim them off if you prefer. Many varieties are only 6 to 8 inches tall. Several other grasses such as little quaking grass, autumn moor grass, and prairie dropseed stay under 12 inches in pots.

Many of the sedges, which are not true grasses, are choice container plants because of their small size. Some grow best submerged in ponds, while others thrive under normal conditions. Other grasslike plants for containers are mondo grass, lilyturf, and dwarf phormiums.

Foliage for Texture and Contrast

Foliage is a constant in all gardens. So crucial is it to the overall structure and character of any planting that it's wise to consider the effects of foliage before thinking of flowers. Where shade predominates, foliage may never give up the spotlight to showier, more colorful blooms. But this doesn't mean that you have to sacrifice beauty or appeal, because foliage gardens are filled with fascinating textures and shapes, light and shadow, and movement and color.

By focusing on these attributes, you can create an exciting center of attention for your container garden. Foliage textures and shapes can range from a weeping Atlas cedar or a fuzzy lamb's ear to a delicate fern frond. Light and shadow play differently on the creamy margins of a cutleaf English ivy and a crinkled hosta leaf. The movement and color of a chartreuse coleus stand in sharp contrast to blue wild rye and purple-leaf geranium. Besides these botanical features, foliage is key for other visual effects as well. Whether spreading or branching, foliage endows container plantings with bulk. And, perhaps most important of all, it provides vertical lines and arching curves that complement the shapes and colors of other plants. ❧

FROM FINE TO BOLD

Leaves with deeply sculptured veins, scalloped or toothlike edges, and contrasting shapes add a deep, rich texture to foliage arrangements in pots. In this planting, the prickly leaves of asparagus fern impart a lacy effect as well. Pale tints can add their own emphasis to foliage texture, besides lighting up shaded sites and dim corners. Variegated foliage is especially valuable when it is multicolored, as it ties the foliage to nearby blooms. ❧

HAVE ON HAND:

- ▶ 14-inch terra-cotta pot
- ▶ Potting mix
- ▶ Pruning shears and scissors
- ▶ Gloves
- ▶ Liquid fertilizer

Plants

- ▶ 1 plectranthus
- ▶ 1 geranium
- ▶ 1 asparagus fern
- ▶ 1 sweet potato vine

Fill a 14-inch-wide terra-cotta container with moist, all-purpose potting mix to within 1 inch of the rim.

Remove plectranthus from its growing pot and place it toward the back of the container. Pinch tips of shoots to encourage bushy growth.

Plant geranium in center, leaving a few inches of space between its foliage and the plectranthus.

Plant asparagus fern in front of geranium. Set rootball at a slight angle, allowing foliage to arch over rim of pot.

Plant sweet potato vine on the other side of the geranium, close to the edge of the pot, so stems drape over it.

Encourage more flowering by snipping old blossoms from geranium. Make cuts at base of flower stems, just above a leaf.

HERE'S HOW

BALANCING SUN AND SHADE

Although foliage plants thrive in shaded sites, most need bright, indirect light for part of the day. Morning sun and filtered afternoon shade are ideal. A deck with overhead protection is often just the right environment, as is a patio area under tall deciduous trees.

Long, spindly stems with leaves widely separated are sure signals that light is inadequate. If you see any of these signs, move the container into brighter light.

Every 2 weeks, clip tips of asparagus fern with sharp scissors to encourage compact growth. Wear gloves to protect against spines.

Every month during the growing season, fertilize the planting with an application of a complete liquid fertilizer such as 15-30-15.

Alternatives

HARMONIOUS FOLIAGE PLANTS

When you begin arranging plants in a container garden, it's natural to begin with the most dominant. This may mean the largest in size, the most distinctive in shape, or the brightest in color. When dealing primarily with foliage, you'll want to balance all these elements. It's easy to combine sizes and shapes, but color can be more challenging. The same organizing principle applies to color—begin with the most dominant shade, then add complementary tones.

Green is generally the first color that comes to mind when we think of foliage. And while you can artfully select and arrange shades of green, splashes of burgundy, bronze, and purple always enhance green, as do sparks of cream, yellow, and gold. Deep tones are impressive at any time while crisp reds and oranges instill dramatic touches, especially in autumn. Chartreuse and lime green never fail to dazzle, whether as soft leaves on a spiraea or as creeping stems on a lysimachia.

You may feel that it's a little risky to arrange just colorful foliage as a star attraction in your garden, but keep in mind that it is a great unifier. Even though one container moves to the foreground, foliage links other elements in your garden.

KOREAN FIR
Abies koreana
15–20 feet tall
Zones 5–7
Small conical tree with pliant branches densely covered with soft green needles. Upright, very attractive purple cones sit atop limbs. Well-drained, acidic to neutral bark-based potting mix; water frequently; full sun.

LAMIUM (DEAD NETTLE)
Lamium maculatum '**White Nancy**'
8–12 inches tall
Zones 3–8
White flowers April to June above silvery white, puckered leaves with green margins; plants trail over edge of pot; standard potting mix; average water; drought tolerant; full/partial shade. 'Pink Pewter' is similar but with pink flowers.

ZEBRA GRASS
Miscanthus sinensis '**Zebrinus**'
3–4 feet tall
Zones 4–9
Vigorous ornamental grass with long, arching leaves. Deep green blades marked with yellow bands. Persistent showy tassels appear above the leaves on strong stalks in late summer. Average potting mix and water; full sun.

CANNA
Canna '**Tropicana**'
4–6 feet tall
Zones 8–11
Warm-climate perennial with lavish, exotic flowers; large paddle-shaped leaves have a tropical look; average potting mix; moderate water; mostly sun to partial shade; lift rhizomes in fall and store in moist peat moss until spring.

MAIDENHAIR FERN
Adiantum spp.
1–2 feet tall
Zones 3–10
Delicate, lacy fronds on wiry stems; thin, fan-shaped leaflets; humus-rich, fast-draining potting mix; keep constantly moist; high humidity; bright shade. Leaves die back in cold weather.

Clever Containers
for Special Spots

Many city dwellers eager to exercise a green thumb aren't able to walk out the back door to a garden bed, but instead find themselves facing structural walls and paved floors. In such situations, the only possible way to create a garden is with containers. And when narrow urban lots and tiny courtyards are the only recourse to flat space, urbanites can rise above their limitations and fashion vertical gardens out of special hanging baskets, wall-mounted pots, and window boxes. In the projects here the usual subjects are ornamentals, but you can just as easily grow herbs and vegetables, too, lifted above the ground.

Rooftop gardens provide some of the best exposure to sunlight in urban areas. Here, you can spread out your containers and diversify plantings to the extent that wind and weight will allow. By adding trees, shrubs, and special flooring, you can create the illusion of a true garden niche. Wooden boxes are good choices for plants on rooftops. They're easy to build on site to fit the garden space. But you may find perfectly good containers by improvising and recycling, and you may even save yourself time and money in the process.

Do-it-yourselfers looking for a unique container will be interested in the final project in this section: a faux stone planter. Miniature plants are well suited to this type of garden trough, which makes a tasteful addition alongside a pool or on a patio. ✤

Building a Tower Garden

You can transform the most unlikely location into an instant garden by planting a flower-covered tower. Its vertical growing surface fits easily into the most limited space, and a tower garden has the added benefits of being simple to move and inexpensive to create.

Plant the tower near your potting bench or in an out-of-the-way work area and wait a few weeks before moving it into prominence, after the small plants have gone through a growth spurt and filled in the tower. As the column fills in, cover any bare spots by making an additional slit in the plastic liner and slipping in another small plant or two so that you end up with a lush and fully covered floral post.

Choose plants that will flourish best in the site where your new vertical garden will grow. Under trees or an overhang, select shade-tolerant species such as impatiens, ferns, ivy, and begonias. In a sunny location, opt for verbena, diascia, tiny daisies, lobelia, and alyssum.

Restricting the tower to just one kind and one color of flowering plant will result in a more streamlined, formal look, while mixing colors and blossom types creates a more fanciful and romantic mood. 🌺

CREATING A VERTICAL GARDEN

Use perlite and fine peat moss for a lightweight potting mix. To cut down on maintenance, mix in slow-release fertilizer.

Use your finger to test moisture at various levels inside the tower, since shaded and exposed areas will dry out unevenly. And be mindful about turning it every few days for even exposure to light. 🌿

HAVE ON HAND:

- 6 x 5-foot plastic-coated steel wire fencing
- Wire cutters
- Duct tape
- Pliers
- Two 5-foot stakes
- Heavy-gauge wire
- Hammer
- Large U-shaped fencing tacks
- 32 x 32-inch plywood base
- Power drill and bits
- Heavy-duty plastic
- Twist ties
- Compost
- Peat moss
- Perlite
- Slow-release fertilizer
- Utility knife
- Mulch

Plants
- Ten 6-packs of petunias

Make a 15-inch-diameter cylinder with the wire fencing. Twist wire ends along seam. Cover ends with duct tape to strengthen and maintain tower.

For garden installation: *Drive 2 stakes into ground about 15 inches apart. Set tower over stakes; secure with heavy-gauge wire.*

For patio, deck, or balcony: *Use U-shaped fencing tacks to fasten to a heavy, wood base. Drill about 5 drainage holes in base.*

Line the inside of the tower with heavy-duty plastic and secure with twist ties wrapped around the wire and through the plastic.

Prepare potting mix of equal parts compost, peat moss, and perlite. Add slow-release fertilizer. Water and blend. Fill tower with mix; tamp lightly.

Starting at bottom, cut slits in plastic 5 inches apart for rootballs. Cut slits in rows 6 inches apart. Stagger holes from one row to the next.

Insert plant rootballs through holes into soil. Angle rootball so the plant points up slightly. Repeat until all slits are filled.

Fill the top of the tower with the remaining plants. Add a layer of mulch to conserve moisture. Water well.

HERE'S HOW

HANGING CONTAINERS

Some hanging containers are sold as a complete unit with a wall bracket and screws, but most are sold separately. To attach a bracket to concrete, brick, or stucco, purchase a special anchor from a hardware store. For wood, use a plain or decorative heavy-duty lag-thread hook. Two-part hooks with a swivel attachment make it easy to turn pots hung in partial shade. To suspend a box, use four screw eyes on the rim or near the corners, and thread through with wire, lightweight chain, or cording.

After you've chosen a spot to hang a container, step back and double-check clearance—underneath, on top, and alongside. As plants grow, they will spread and dangle at least a foot in all directions.

Alternatives

HANGING POTS

The simplest version of a hanging garden is a single pot filled with just one kind of plant. Let your outdoor architecture and exposure to sun or shade determine how to display your hanging garden and what types of plants to choose. A sunny patio wall, for example, is a perfect spot for zonal geraniums, trailing petunias, or Mexican daisies. Despite heat and reflected light, these plants bloom in bright, long-lasting colors. Hang plastic pots from extended wall brackets or overhead supports. For a more artistic arrangement, suspend simple clay pots in nearly invisible rings to create a three-dimensional tableau that appears to float over the background. Complete your picture by color coordinating the perky blossoms with other nearby container plants and outdoor furniture.

Small containers in sunny sites dry out fast and call for daily watering in most climates. Your plants will do best if you start them out in a humus-rich potting mix fortified with water-retentive polymers to carry them through the hottest, driest weather. In mild winters or while waiting for warm days in early spring, plant a hardier species, such as cascading, fragrant violas or vibrant pansies. 🌸

HANGING GARDENS

A container that is suspended several feet above the ground may trick the eye into visually expanding a garden space, but more importantly, it provides you with another place to grow a favorite plant. Hanging gardens can be fast and easy with a single flowering plant, or they can be intricate combinations of foliage with annuals and perennials that bloom from spring through fall. The best are planted with draping and trailing species that carry blossoms through multiple seasons.

When choosing a container take into consideration how quickly it will lose moisture. Wood and plastic are often recommended because they dry out more slowly than terra cotta and wire baskets, but when hanging, even pots of these materials must be watered more frequently than when on the ground. Unless you custom-design an automated system, watering usually results in spills and drips, so check the area, especially the floor, for durability. Another consideration is weight. Whether you hang containers on walls or fences, under arbors or eaves, or from posts and pergolas, the attachment and the hanger must be sturdy. Be prepared to drill into walls or beams to anchor a support. 🌸

Window Boxes

The secret to a dynamic window box lies in careful planning and dedication to its upkeep. As with any kind of gardening, it is always tempting to look for shortcuts but generally hard to find them. With window boxes, however, you can cut a few corners and still end up with a fabulous display.

Instead of planting a box in the traditional method, fill it with small pots holding mature plants in full bloom. Because this approach takes some planning to give the appearance of a unified arrangement, it works best to custom-make a box to fit the exact dimensions of your pots. Coordinate your design with the exterior of your home so that it blends with the window trim and other architectural features.

Have plenty of replacement plants on hand to pop into your window box as soon as one group of plants begins to lose its freshness or you just want a change for the season. The advantage here is twofold. First, you have the convenience of substituting one plant for another without going through the messy transplanting process at the window. And second, you don't have to wait while small plants grow to size before enjoying spring bulbs, summer annuals, and vibrant autumn colors, each in turn. ✿

A TWIG WINDOW BOX

A lightweight twig planter makes a quick, easy, and inexpensive project that adds a rustic note to any garden scene. The pots themselves will be on view in this open-sided box, so be sure to scrub them clean before planting.

HAVE ON HAND:

- Circular power saw or hand saw
- Seven 27-inch lengths of 1½-inch-diameter beech or similar wood
- Ten 11-inch lengths of 1½-inch-diameter beech or similar wood
- Tape measure
- Pencil
- Safety glasses
- Carpenter's square
- Ribbed drywall nails
- Power drill and ⅛-inch bit
- Hammer
- Three 6-inch terra-cotta pots
- Sphagnum moss

Plants
- Bedding plants (seasonal)

Using 1½-inch-diameter beech or similar wood, cut 7 pieces 27 inches long and 10 pieces 11 inches long.

For bottom, place 3 long pieces parallel and 3 inches apart. Set a short piece atop these at each end to form a rectangle.

Drill holes ¾ inch from ends of short pieces into long sections beneath. Nail pieces together with ribbed drywall nails.

Measure 8 inches from both ends and place 2 short pieces across long pieces on marks. Drill holes and join as in Step 3.

Set 2 long pieces atop the short pieces, directly above the long pieces beneath. Drill holes and join as in Step 3.

Place 4 short pieces atop the long pieces, directly above the short pieces beneath. Join as in Step 3.

Attach the remaining 2 short pieces to back of box at each end. Nail through these extensions to hang. Top with 2 long sections and join.

Place three 6-inch clay pots planted with geraniums or other seasonal blooms in box. Fill around pots with sphagnum moss.

HERE'S HOW

AVOID MOISTURE DAMAGE

Avoid trapped moisture and structural damage behind a window box by providing ample space for air circulation. If you use steel L-brackets as a mounting device, fit a spacer behind the box or behind each bracket as you attach it. If you use decorative wood supports, use material at least 2 inches thick.

To slow down deterioration in the interior of a wood box, fit it with a pre-formed liner or a sheet of heavy-duty plastic before planting. Be sure to cut drainage holes above those in the window box. Fit the liner carefully into the corners, fill with potting mix, and position all the plants before trimming. Leave a little excess plastic over the rim, then tuck it inside for a neatly finished edge.

Alternatives

TRADITIONAL WINDOW BOX

A vibrant window display sends a cheery message to passersby outside and brightens the indoor rooms, too. Flowers and foliage with strong colors provide a focal point on a building exterior, especially when hues mimic window trim, decorative shutters, or other architectural features.

Though you may want to delve right into planting a window box, it's prudent to take an overview before beginning. Be sure that you will have easy access through the window to your box, as it's easier to maintain from the inside than from out-of-doors. Consider also how it will be supported. Wood or steel brackets below the window make the best braces, but many boxes can rest on a window ledge and be secured to the trim. Drainage issues can be a bit more challenging in window boxes than in other container gardens. The box must hold enough moisture for crowded groups of plants, yet excess water should drain away freely without dripping on passersby below or damaging your house. On window ledges, set the box on a drip tray. Check conditions above your box, too, such as the gutters and the roof overhang. Runoff after heavy storms can dislodge and ruin your plants. 🌺

DECORATED BOXES

You can find window boxes in an amazing variety of sizes and shapes. It's no wonder, since we find them decorating everything from fire escapes and storefronts to porch railings and doorsteps. Many of these are plain, painted wood, while some are elaborately adorned. Depending on how you plant your box, only a small part of the exterior may be visible—or none at all—during most of the season. If you store your boxes over winter, you may be satisfied with a plain design. But if your box remains in view year-round or if your plantings are streamlined or nontrailing, consider adding decorative touches.

You can give your wood box any number of ornamental finishes, such as molded shapes, beading strips, or bamboo tacked over the front panel. For a nicely finished look, place a cap over the top edge and a piece of trim around the bottom. And you can always work wonders with a coat of paint. For a designer look, add embellishments with the second coat: Rag swirls impart a marbled look, metallic additives applied with a blunt brush make gilt stippling, and a stenciled design can fit whatever style you wish, from folk to high Victorian. 🌺

Rooftop Gardens

City dwellers who want to garden are lucky if they have access to a rooftop. Although they must deal with wind and smog on a regular basis, they gain sunlight and space. It takes some dedication to set up a high-rise garden, since all materials have to be lugged up stairs or on an elevator. Before toting and installing all the containers, make some initial arrangements. Check first with the building superintendent or the architect about the structural support and how much weight different areas will bear. The weight of even small containers adds up when they're filled with soil and water. Just one 10-foot tree in a box 24 inches wide by 24 inches deep is amazingly heavy, over 300 pounds. An entire collection of plants calls for special placement over load-bearing walls.

Take a full survey of other needs, too, before beginning. Inquire about drainage, security, and, of course, water. All plants must be irrigated, since rainfall is never adequate for containers in wind and full sun. Choose plants that do well in containers and tolerate tough environmental conditions, too, such as air pollution and sudden and severe fluctuations in weather. ❀

HIGH-RISE GARDENING

Geraniums and mums can take more exposure than impatiens, which need protection against wind and sun. Set impatiens at the base of a shrub or in nooks and corners. Use bright colors in large pots and on flowering trees to stand out against the competing vista or skyline.

Rain alone rarely provides enough moisture, so check soil often, even if you use an automatic irrigation system.

HAVE ON HAND:

- ▶ 16- to 18-inch container
- ▶ Four or five 8-inch pots
- ▶ Two 8 x 30-inch planters
- ▶ Potting mix
- ▶ Topsoil
- ▶ Sand
- ▶ Automatic drip irrigation system

Plants

- ▶ Japanese aucuba or Siberian cypress
- ▶ 4–5 chrysanthemums
- ▶ 12–15 geraniums
- ▶ 10–12 impatiens

Use large, heavy containers for trees. Fill with potting mix supplemented with topsoil and sand so plants won't blow over.

In sheltered locations: You can plant trees in plastic pots to reduce weight. Place containers on wheeled dollies for easy transport.

In shaded areas: Plant shrubs with variegated leaves and shade-loving plants such as Japanese aucuba and Siberian cypress.

Plant four or five 8-inch-diameter pots with chrysanthemums or other daisylike flowers. Arrange in a cluster at base of trees.

Plant pink, white, or red geraniums in 8-inch-diameter pots, 3 to a pot. Set pots in groups of 3 around garden.

Fill long, narrow planters with potting mix. Plant them with impatiens. Set them along the front edge of the garden.

Every few days, remove dead leaves and faded blossoms from plants. Collect clippings in a container and discard.

To both conserve water and provide continual watering, set up a drip irrigation system, with an emitter in each pot.

HERE'S HOW

WINTER PROTECTION

Container plants suffer in cold climates because their rootballs are exposed on all sides. Conversely, they thaw faster, too, producing alternate freezing and thawing that can damage roots. A lining of insulating packing nuggets, Styrofoam sheeting, or other insulated material reduces the problem, but it also helps to blanket containers in bubble wrap on the outside.

Containers themselves can also be damaged as water-laden soil expands inside and exerts pressure against the walls. Damage is just as common when moisture inside porous materials freezes and expands, causing pots to crack and break. Terra cotta is the most vulnerable. To prevent breakage, remove plants from clay pots and store empty pots upside down or move pots inside until the return of warmer temperatures.

Alternatives

LOW-MAINTENANCE URBAN GARDEN

Full sun, wind, and poor air quality present quite a challenge for both the rooftop gardener and container plants. By selecting known survivors in tough conditions, you'll be on your way to success right from the start. A good number of trees, shrubs, annuals, and perennials thrive under buffeting winds and scorching conditions that dry out pots and plants. Pine, cypress, and juniper are trees that take less care on a daily basis but hold up in the long run in containers.

While trees provide the most screening, you may want to fill in with ivies and flowering vines on trellises and easy-care shrubs that need little trimming. Boxwood, false holly, forsythia, and nandina withstand wind and stress, as do tough, shrublike plants like agave and phormium. Besides functioning as privacy walls, these taller species also make attractive backgrounds for lower-growing plants. Flowering annuals may be your first choice for plants in smaller pots, but try including slender-leaved, mounding perennials and grasses that adapt well to rooftop conditions. If you must have a rose, 'Buff Beauty', 'Carefree Wonder', and 'Stanwell Perpetual' are three that don't seem to suffer under environmental stress. 🌾

WINTERCREEPER
Euonymus fortunei **'Emerald Gaiety'**
3–5 feet tall
Zones 5–9
Compact, mounding shrub with bright green leaves edged with white; foliage tinged with pink in winter; standard potting mix; average to low water; full/partial sun; will climb if supported on wall or trellis.

HETZ JUNIPER
Juniperus **'Hetzii Columnaris'**
8–12 feet tall
Zones 3–9
Conical evergreen with bright green needles touched with bluish frost; reddish brown, peeling bark; moderately fast grower; average potting mix; moderate water; full sun. Tolerates heat and drought.

MUGO PINE
Pinus mugo
5–10 feet tall
Zones 3–7
Slow-growing, shrubby evergreen tree of variable form; upturned branches give plant a rounded shape; short, dark green needles; small cones; soil-based potting mix; average to low water; full sun.

BROOM
Cytisus scoparius **'Moonlight'**
30 inches tall
Zones 5–8
Compact variety with pale yellow pealike flowers; slender, arching stems; small leaves on woody shrub; a tough survivor; standard potting mix; low water; full sun. Prune just to shape after bloom.

AGAVE
Agave americana **'Marginata'**
2–6 feet tall
Zones 10–11
Succulent native to Mexico producing rosette of large, fleshy, sword-shaped leaves barbed with down-curved thorns. Leaves are edged with butter yellow margins. Fast-draining, sandy potting mix; water sparingly; full sun.

Building a Wooden Planter

Wood planters fill more than one role in the container garden scene. They can be designed to blend with outdoor décor; they withstand the rigors of winter in cold climates; and they can be built economically with little effort. This is good news, because you may need to custom-make a box to accommodate a tree or shrub if you're unable to find a suitable pot.

The design here is spacious enough to hold a small tree, but by altering the dimensions, you can build this simple box to suit several purposes. Scale it down for flowering plants, lengthen it for a hedge, or make several and fill them with trees for a formal row of evenly matched plants. Wood boxes also make excellent containers for vegetables. Unadorned ones are simple substitutes for raised beds in the backyard, but with the added trim shown here, vegetable containers can move onto the patio or grace the front entry.

To slow down deterioration inside the planter, you may want to line it with plastic. Be sure to cut drainage holes in the liner to correspond with those in the bottom of the box. By using heavy-duty plastic with no drainage holes, you can even convert your planter into a miniature water garden. ✤

A SQUARE WOOD CONTAINER

To preserve rich wood tones, apply a nontoxic preservative each year to the exterior. Left unfinished, it will develop a gray patina from weathering. If you paint the planter, choose a color that will complement foliage and blossoms. Use one coat of primer, then one or two coats of exterior paint.

HAVE ON HAND:

- Four 2 x 4s, 24 inches long
- Four 2 x 4s, 22¼ inches long
- 3-inch flathead wood screws
- Power drill and ³⁄₁₆-inch bit
- Tape measure
- Pencil
- Carpenter's square
- Safety goggles
- Four 2 x 2s, 24 inches long
- Five 5 x 8 tongue-and-groove cedar paneling, 24 inches long
- 1½-inch finish nails
- Nail set
- Miter box and saw
- 1 x 5 x 8-inch cedar board
- Corner molding, 8 feet long
- Quarter round molding, 8 feet long

Make one frame for top and one for bottom, 24 inches square, from 2 x 4 lumber. Drill pilot holes and join pieces with wood screws.

Attach 24-inch lengths of 2 x 2 lumber to form inside corners. Drill pilot holes and join with wood screws to form square planter box.

Sheath sides with tongue-and-groove cedar paneling. Attach with finish nails. Be sure corners are flush.

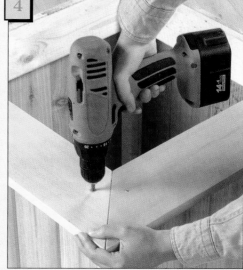

For sill, screw 1 x 5 board along top edges; miter corners. Nail corner molding to corners and quarter round molding under top strip and along base.

A Faux Stone Planting Trough

Once used as barnyard waterers, stone troughs have journeyed far since they left their humble origins to enter the gardening world.

This project shows how to fashion a planting trough that looks like stone but is lightweight and inexpensive and therefore easier to use than the heavy originals. After your trough weathers for a season or two, it will look even more like real stone. Add plantings of succulents, miniatures, and specialty rock garden or alpine plants, and your trough will look as if it has been part of the landscape for centuries.

A plastic crate is just one kind of form you can use to fashion a trough. Wood, a cardboard box, or an old porcelain or metal sink will work nearly as well. You may want to try a free-form bowl by pressing the hypertufa mix over a mound of sand in any shape. Other options include adding fiberglass shreds to strengthen the hypertufa and mixing in a concrete colorant that will help blend the planter with other landscape features.

You can also mold matching hypertufa supports for your trough to elevate it for better drainage and make decorative hypertufa rocks as accents.

WORKING WITH HYPERTUFA

When planning the dimensions, consider where you will be using the trough. A small box shape is well suited for patios and decks, and you can move it easily. Flatter, longer troughs accommodate more plants, but the soil dries out faster. Unless you use only drought-tolerant species, the plants will require frequent attention. 🌺

HAVE ON HAND:

- 18 x 24-inch plastic storage box
- Heavy-duty plastic
- Perlite
- Portland cement
- Peat moss
- Five 2-inch dowels, ¾ inch in diameter
- 14 x 20-inch plastic shoe storage box
- Masonry trowel
- Plastic wrap
- Stiff wire brush
- Screwdriver or file
- Potting mix

Plants
- 5–6 assorted miniature or alpine species

Prepare the larger plastic storage box by lining it with heavy-duty plastic, allowing 2 or 3 inches to overlap around the top edge.

Combine 1 part perlite, 1 part Portland cement, and 2 parts peat moss. Add water gradually until mixture is like very dry cottage cheese.

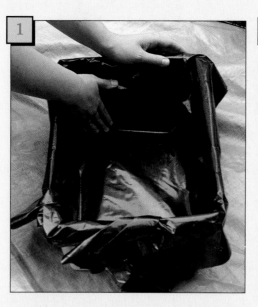

Spread a 2-inch layer of mixture in bottom of box. Push five 2-inch dowels vertically into mix, evenly spaced and at least 2 inches from sides.

Center the shoe storage box over the mix. Fill the area between the boxes with mix, tamping as you work.

Smooth top edges with masonry trowel. Cover with plastic wrap and allow trough to sit and cure until dry (about 3 or 4 days).

When mixture no longer gives when pressed with a finger, remove plastic containers. Push dowels out.

Brush sides with a stiff wire brush to add texture. Score with a file or screwdriver for a more antique look, if you wish.

Fill trough with fast-draining potting mix. Plant with miniature or alpine species that grow slowly so they don't quickly outgrow the container.

HERE'S HOW

HYPERTUFA ACCESSORIES

To make your new trough even more like an authentic stone trough, set it on matching supports made out of the same hypertufa mixture. Simply form two rectangular blocks approximately the height of bricks but as wide as your new planter. Allow them to dry thoroughly before resting the trough on top.

After your trough is planted, accessorize it with small pieces of driftwood or hypertufa rocks. Make the rocks out of the same mixture as for the trough, but smooth the surface so that little peat is revealed. Mold the rocks by hand or inside a plastic bag. Before they dry completely, form depressions or sculpt ridges on the surface of the rocks.

Alternatives

MINIATURE PLANTS FOR TROUGHS

A trough itself is as fascinating as the plants that go inside it, and this is one of the great advantages. You will be drawn to a trough more frequently than to other containers, and in the process, you'll have greater opportunity to observe the plants carefully. In a trough, you can gather tiny species that would get lost in the ground or in small pots set off somewhere by themselves. And in one spot, it's easy to set up a temporary cover for shade or protection from excess rain and cold.

Let the plants themselves determine where you site your trough. Sun-loving succulents and alpines will languish in shade. In an unprotected site, wind and reflected sunlight from a wall or concrete floor can dry out the container faster than you might expect. Pets and children may treat specialty plants with too little respect in high-traffic areas.

The trough is an ideal container for plants that need special drainage. A gritty potting mix, small-sized gravel spread over the surface, and careful watering should also be a part of their care and maintenance. Be sure to test the soil for moisture a few inches below the surface before watering.

LEWISIA
Lewisia cotyledon 'Alba'
6–10 inches
Zones 5–8
Rosettes of spoon-shaped evergreen leaves and white flowers from spring through summer; very well-drained, neutral to slightly acidic soil of equal parts sand, peat moss, and compost; light shade; average water.

PETER PAN SAXIFRAGE
Saxifraga 'Peter Pan'
3–6 inches
Zones 5–7
Clump-forming plant with tiny, mosslike foliage; dainty rose-pink flowers in late spring to summer; very well-drained soil of sand or gravel, peat moss, and compost; keep moist; full sun in cool climates, light shade in warmer regions.

LEPTINELLA
Leptinella squalida
3–6 inches
Zones 4–7
Creeping, mat-forming perennial with small, ferny foliage; yellowish, ball-shaped flower heads on slender stalks in late spring to early summer; well-drained, moist soil; full sun; few pests.

PINK
Dianthus 'Tiny Rubies'
3–5 inches
Zones 5–8
Low-growing perennial with slender, grayish green foliage; bears abundant small, sweetly fragrant, sparkling red blossoms in spring; mulch with gravel or stone to avoid fungal diseases; well-drained, neutral to alkaline potting mix; average water; full sun.

KAMCHATKA STONECROP
Sedum kamtschaticum 'Variegatum'
2–4 inches
Zones 4–9
Low-growing perennial with shiny, medium green leaves edged in white; starlike yellow flowers from summer to early fall; petals turn reddish with age; well-drained, neutral to slightly alkaline soil with compost and sand; average water; full sun.

Glossary

ACCENT a feature providing a focal point or calling attention to some special aspect of a garden design.

ANNUAL a plant that completes its life cycle (sprouts from seed, grows, flowers, sets seed, and dies) within one growing season.

BARK MULCH processed organic mulch made from the bark of trees, usually conifers.

BULB a compact, underground, thickened stem containing a bud and stored nutrients, all encased in fleshy scales or a thin sheath.

BULBLIKE PLANTS plants that grow from specialized underground stem structures similar to bulbs, but botanically are corms, rhizomes, tubers, and tuberous roots.

CANOPY the leafy crown of a tree.

COMPOST partially decayed organic material, usually from plants, that improves soil structure, texture, and fertility.

CONIFER a tree or shrub that often has needle-like evergreen foliage and bears naked seeds enclosed within a cone or conelike structure.

COOL-SEASON PLANT a plant that grows most vigorously in spring or fall when temperatures range between 50° and 70°F.

CORM a bulblike structure composed of a swollen underground stem that develops roots from a basal plate. A new corm forms on top of the old one each year. Examples of corms are freesia and gladiolus.

COTTAGE GARDEN an informal combination of annuals and perennials, often gracing the front entry of a home.

CULTIVAR one of a group of plants selected and propagated for a particular characteristic, such as flower color or height. Cultivar names are always given in single quotes (as in *Nierembergia* 'Purple Robe').

DEADHEADING removing spent flowers before they produce seeds. Done to stimulate further bloom, to conserve plant strength, and to maintain a tidy appearance.

DECIDUOUS a plant that drops its leaves for part of the year and produces new foliage after a period of dormancy.

DORMANCY a condition marked by the absence of vegetative growth.

DWARF a plant smaller in stature and scale than others of its species or type.

EDGING a row of plants around the rim of a container for visual interest.

ESPALIER training plants to grow with a two-dimensional appearance, such as growing against a flat surface.

EVERGREEN a plant that holds its foliage for more than one year.

FOLIAGE PLANT a plant grown for leaf shape, size, texture, and color to supply bulk and contrast in the garden.

FORMAL a garden style defined by symmetry and balance where plants are highly managed to appear orderly and controlled.

GROUND COVER any low-growing plant used to cover the potting soil and act as a living mulch.

HARDINESS a plant's ability to survive all the variables of a certain climate.

HEAVING the upward movement of soil caused by alternate freezing and thawing.

HUMUS decomposed organic matter added to soil to improve its ability to hold water and air. Compost, peat moss, rotted manure, and leaf mold are examples that are often blended into a potting mix.

HYBRID a plant produced by crossing genetically different plants of a genetically similar group, such as a species.

HYPERTUFA a mixture of lightweight materials, concrete, and water that can be molded into imitation rocks or trough planters.

INFORMAL a garden style where plants are allowed to develop natural form within a natural-looking design.

LAVA ROCK porous, lightweight material of volcanic origin that is added to potting mixes to prevent compaction, especially in containers for trees and shrubs.

LEAF MOLD partially decomposed leaves.

MULCH any material spread over the soil surface to retain soil moisture, moderate soil temperature, suppress weed growth, and improve the garden's appearance.

NODE the point where a bud, leaf, or branch is attached to a stem.

NONPOROUS materials such as plastic and glazed clay that are unable to absorb moisture or allow air to filter through.

ORGANIC MATTER material such as compost derived from decomposed plants or animals.

PEAT MOSS various types of sphagnum moss used as a soil amendment.

PERENNIAL a plant that can live for more than two growing seasons.

PERLITE a white volcanic material expanded by heat into kernels that hold water and nutrients and prevent compaction in potting mixes.

PINCHING a technique using the thumb and forefinger to remove a shoot tip, generally to encourage a plant to produce bushier growth.

POROUS materials such as terra cotta and wood that allow air and water to penetrate.

POTTING MIX a blend of organic and inorganic materials that foster root growth in containers. Does not necessarily contain actual soil, but is often referred to as "potting soil."

PUMICE a lightweight volcanic material similar to lava rock that holds moisture and prevents compaction in containers.

RHIZOME a specialized stem, often horizontal, from which new plants rise.

ROOTBALL the mass of roots and potting soil visible when you remove a plant from its pot.

ROOT PRUNING the process of trimming roots from the outside of a rootball to restrict plant growth or provide space in a container for potting mix, air, and water.

ROOT ZONE the area within a container where roots grow.

SHEARING removing the outer growing tips of a plant to create a uniform height or shape. Usually done with hedge clippers.

SOIL POLYMERS superabsorbent gels that can be added to a potting mix for their ability to hold many times their weight in water and release it slowly into the root zone as the soil dries out.

SPECIES in scientific classification, the category below genus composed of genetically similar plants that can freely breed.

SPECIMEN a single plant placed prominently for its ornamental effect; often a focal point.

SPHAGNUM MOSS a type of coarse peat moss valued for its moisture-retentive ability, especially as a mulch in containers or a liner for wire baskets.

SPREADING growth that extends horizontally as branches elongate.

STAKING reinforcing a weak-stemmed plant by tying it to a strong, upright support.

STANDARD a plant trained to grow as a single, leafless stem topped with a bushy "head."

TENDERNESS a plant's susceptibility to damage by frost.

THINNING removing branches or stems to allow more air and light to reach the interior of a plant.

TOPIARY an artful form created by training or pruning plants to resemble animals and geometric shapes.

TUBER a usually swollen, underground stem base that stores plant food, has buds, and develops roots; examples of tubers are cyclamen and some begonias.

TUBEROUS ROOTS tubers produced from roots, rather than stems; an example of a plant with tuberous roots is dahlia.

VARIEGATION foliage with contrasting markings or margins.

VERMICULITE a lightweight, flaky material produced by exposing mica to high temperatures; often added to potting mix to improve both water retention and drainage.

WARM-SEASON PLANT a plant that grows most vigorously in summer or when temperatures rise above 70°F.

Index

Time-Life Books is a division of Time Life Inc.
Time-Life is a trademark of Time Warner Inc. and affiliated companies.

TIME LIFE INC.
CHAIRMAN AND CHIEF EXECUTIVE OFFICER: Jim Nelson
PRESIDENT AND CHIEF OPERATING OFFICER: Steven Janas
SENIOR EXECUTIVE VICE PRESIDENT AND CHIEF OPERATIONS OFFICER:
   Mary Davis Holt
SENIOR VICE PRESIDENT AND CHIEF FINANCIAL OFFICER: Christopher Hearing

TIME-LIFE BOOKS
PRESIDENT: Larry Jellen
SENIOR VICE PRESIDENT, NEW MARKETS: Bridget Boel
VICE PRESIDENT, HOME AND HEARTH MARKETS: Nicholas M. DiMarco
VICE PRESIDENT, CONTENT DEVELOPMENT: Jennifer L. Pearce

TIME-LIFE TRADE PUBLISHING
VICE PRESIDENT AND PUBLISHER: Neil S. Levin
SENIOR SALES DIRECTOR: Richard J. Vreeland
DIRECTOR, MARKETING AND PUBLICITY: Inger Forland
DIRECTOR OF TRADE SALES: Dana Hobson
DIRECTOR OF CUSTOM PUBLISHING: John Lalor
DIRECTOR OF RIGHTS AND LICENSING: Olga Vezeris

CONTAINER GARDENS
DIRECTOR OF NEW PRODUCT DEVELOPMENT: Carolyn M. Clark
NEW PRODUCT DEVELOPMENT MANAGER: Lori A. Woehrle
SENIOR EDITOR: Linda Bellamy
DIRECTOR OF DESIGN: Kate L. McConnell
PROJECT EDITOR: Jennie Halfant
TECHNICAL SPECIALIST: Monika Lynde
PAGE MAKEUP SPECIALIST: Jennifer Gearhart
DIRECTOR OF PRODUCTION: Carolyn Bounds
QUALITY ASSURANCE: Jim King and Stacy L. Eddy

Printed in U.S.A.
10 9 8 7 6 5 4 3 2 1

Produced by Storey Communications, Inc.
Pownal, Vermont

President	Pamela B. Art
Director of Custom Publishing	Megan Kuntze
Editorial Director	Margaret J. Lydic
Project Manager	Gwen W. Steege
Book Editor	Molly T. Jackel
Horticultural Editor	Charles W.G. Smith
Photo Coordination	Giles Prett, Cici Mulder, Erik Callahan
Book Design	Jonathon Nix/Verso Design
Art Direction	Mark A. Tomasi
Production and Layout	Jennifer A. Jepson Smith
Indexer	Susan Olason, Indexes and Knowledge Maps
Author	Rosemary McCreary
Primary Photography	Kevin Kennefick

Additional photography on pages, as follows: ©Walter Chandoha (16, 73 left, 91 left,
126); Crandall & Crandall (32, 52); Rosalind Creasy (44); ©Alan & Linda Detrick
(51 right, 69 left, 69 right, 112, 122, 130); ©Ken Druse (47 right, 63 left, 100, 122 right);
Thomas E. Eltzroth (35 right, 43 right, 47 left, 85 right, 125 left); ©Derek Fell (iv, v, 36,
40, 43 right, 63 right, 64-65, 81 right, 92, 125 right); Roger Foley (39 right, 86-87);
GardenIMAGE/John Glover (26-27); GardenIMAGE/Martien Uinkesteijn (35 left, 74);
Harry Haralambou (111 left); Holt Studios International (28, 55, 107 right); Donna and
Tom Krischan (6-7); P. Lindtner (56, 60, 118); Janet Loughrey (31 right); Allan Mandell
(66, 70, 73 right, 88, 95 right, 96, 132); J. Paul Moore (8, 48, 91 right, 104, 108); Jerry
Pavia (31 left, 39 right, 78, 82, 85 left, 111 right); Positive Images/Karen Bussolini (51
left); Positive Images/Jerry Howard (81 right); H. Armstrong Roberts/A. Hubrick (116-
117, 121 right); Patricia A. Taylor (95 left); Chuck Weight (107 left).

Special thanks to the following for their help: Berkshire Botanic Gardens, Stockbridge,
MA; California Redwood Association, Novato, CA; Collector's Warehouse,
Williamstown, MA; Ward's Nursery and Garden Center, Great Barrington, MA.

School and library distribution by Time-Life Education, P.O. Box 85026,
Richmond, Virginia 23285-5026.

CIP data available upon request:
Librarian, Time-Life Books
2000 Duke Street
Alexandria, Virginia 22314

ISBN 0-7370-0624-2

Zone Map

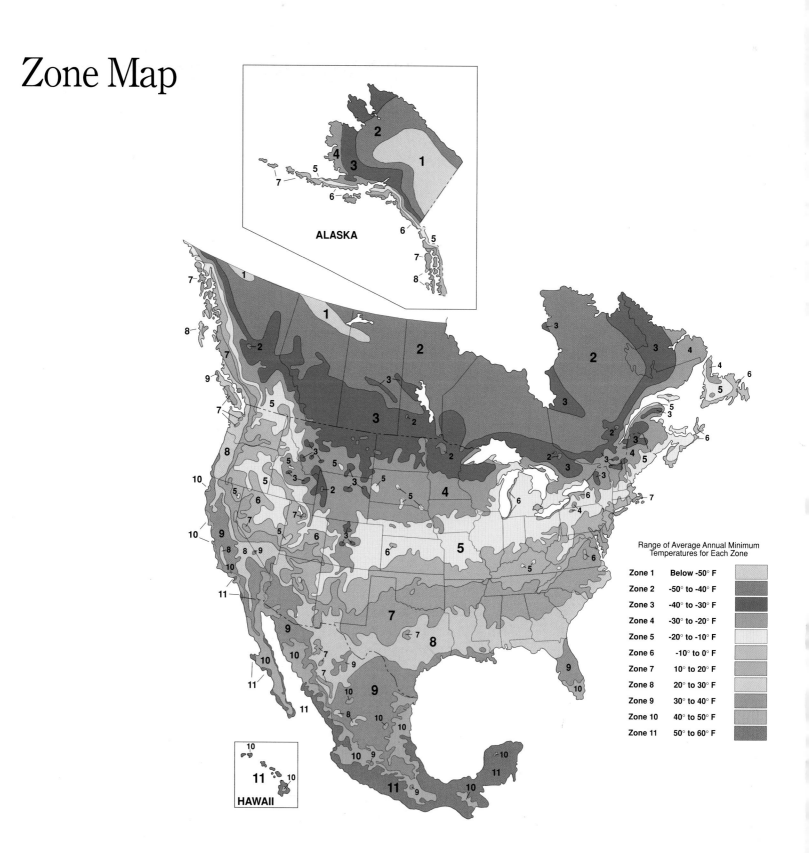

ALASKA

HAWAII

Range of Average Annual Minimum
Temperatures for Each Zone

Zone 1	**Below -50° F**
Zone 2	**-50° to -40° F**
Zone 3	**-40° to -30° F**
Zone 4	**-30° to -20° F**
Zone 5	**-20° to -10° F**
Zone 6	**-10° to 0° F**
Zone 7	**10° to 20° F**
Zone 8	**20° to 30° F**
Zone 9	**30° to 40° F**
Zone 10	**40° to 50° F**
Zone 11	**50° to 60° F**